The ⁱⁱⁱ
and
Old Violin Makers

Also from Westphalia Press

westphaliapress.org

The Idea of the Digital University

Bulwarks Against Poverty in America

Treasures of London

Avate Garde Politician

L'Enfant and the Freemasons

Baronial Bedrooms

Making Trouble for Muslims

Philippine Masonic Directory ~ 1918

Paddle Your Own Canoe

Opportunity and Horatio Alger

Careers in the Face of Challenge

Bookplates of the Kings

Hymns to the Gods

Freemasonry in Old Buffalo

Original Cables from the Pearl Harbor Attack

Social Satire and the Modern Novel

The Essence of Harvard

The Genius of Freemasonry

A Definitive Commentary on Bookplates

James Martineau and Rebuilding Theology

Bohemian San Francisco

The Wizard

Crime 3.0

Anti-Masonry and the Murder of Morgan

Understanding Art

Spies I Knew

Lodge "Himalayan Brotherhood" No. 459 C.E.

Ancient Masonic Mysteries

Collecting Old Books

Masonic Secret Signs and Passwords

Death Valley in '49

Lariats and Lassos

Mr. Garfield of Ohio

The Wisdom of Thomas Starr King

The French Foreign Legion

War in Syria

Naturism Comes to the United States

New Sources on Women and Freemasonry

Designing, Adapting, Strategizing in Online Education

Gunboat and Gun-runner

Memoirs of a Poor Relation

Espionage!

Bohemian San Francisco

Tales of Old Japan

The Violin and Old Violin Makers

A Historical & Biographical Account of the Violin

by A. Mason Clarke

WESTPHALIA PRESS
An imprint of Policy Studies Organization

Westphalia Press
An imprint of Policy Studies Organization
1527 New Hampshire Ave., NW
Washington, D.C. 20036
info@ipsonet.org

ISBN-13: 978-1-63391-089-8
ISBN-10: 163391089X

Cover design by Taillefer Long at Illuminated Stories:
www.illuminatedstories.com

Daniel Gutierrez-Sandoval, Executive Director
PSO and Westphalia Press

Rahima Schwenkbeck, Director of Marketing and Media
PSO and Westphalia Press

Updated material and comments on this edition
can be found at the Westphalia Press website:
www.westphaliapress.org

THE VIOLIN AND OLD VIOLIN MAKERS.

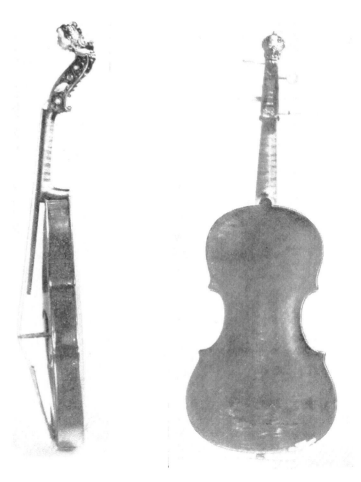

A COPY OF THE GASPARO DA SALO VIOLIN USED BY OLE BULL, THE
FAMOUS SCANDINAVIAN VIOLINIST, MADE BY MR. GILLINGHAM, OF
CHISWICK. (*The front view of this violin will be
found on the cover.*)

THE VIOLIN

AND

OLD VIOLIN MAKERS

BEING A

HISTORICAL & BIOGRAPHICAL

ACCOUNT OF THE VIOLIN

With Facsimiles of Labels
of the Old Makers

BY

A. MASON CLARKE

[AUTHOR OF "BIOGRAPHICAL DICTIONARY OF FIDDLERS."]

LONDON :
WILLIAM REEVES, 83 CHARING CROSS ROAD, W.C.
Publisher of Books on Music.

COPY OF GASPARO DA SALO

(SEE FRONTISPIECE)

PREFACE.

THIS little work is the outcome of some little thought, born of hesitation. To be clear, I should mention that some years ago I completed a somewhat exhaustive work on the violin, the first portion of which reached the stereotype stage, but unfortunately owing to a fire the plates were destroyed. Other business pressing, the work was laid aside. In the meantime other books on the violin have been published, a fact which might be taken as rendering any further work on the subject superfluous. However, it has been suggested to me by some musical friends that if I could produce a popular work which could be issued at a low price it would be well received. Buoyed up with this hope, I set to work with the object of presenting in a concise form such information as I have thought necessary or at least of interest to every one who elects to take up the violin, either as an object of recreation or serious study. Time alone will prove whether or not the appearance of this addition to the literature of the violin is justified.

In order to facilitate my labours I have consulted the leading British and foreign authorities on the violin and kindred instruments. I have also during many years devoted much time to the inspection and study of genuine old instruments.

Λ. M. C.

FOREST HILL, LONDON.

CONTENTS.

PART I.

HISTORICAL.

	PAGES
I.—Introductory and Early English ...	1-29
II.—Italy ...	30-35
III.—France ...	36-40
IV.—Germany ...	41-44

PART II.

BIOGRAPHICAL.

VIOLIN MAKERS OF THE OLD SCHOOLS.

I.—Italian, with Labels	45-71
II.—German and Tyrolese, with Labels	72-82
III.—French, with Labels	83-89
IV.—British, with Label ...	90-103

PART III.

On the Development of Classical Music for the Violin and other Stringed Instruments   ... 105-117

Frontispiece: A Copy of the Gasparo da Salo Violin used by Ole Bull, the famous Scandinavian violinist. Made by Mr. Gillingham, of Chiswick.

PART I.

HISTORICAL.

I.—INTRODUCTORY AND EARLY ENGLISH.

THE origin of the violin is always a very interesting subject for study. It is one upon which many great writers have devoted much time and thought, but as they arrive at varying conclusions, and in some cases opposite opinions, the result is to leave the mind of the student in a state of conjecture and speculation.

In tracing the development of certain species of stringed instruments the arguments of some authorities often appear pretty conclusive, but generally we are confronted with such a mass of contradictory assertions, that we can only treat the theories put

forward as approximate. The professor, teacher
and matured student approaching this subject, of
course do so with great profit, as they are better
able to accept or reject whatever may be said concerning the ancestry of the violin family, than is
the young beginner.

For those who desire a more extended knowledge
of the rise and progress of the violin family a large
field of literature is open. As a preparatory the
author recommends Otto's " Treatise on the Struc-
ture and Preservation of the Violin" (W. Reeves,
London), which contains much valuable and interesting information on the subject.

Now, there can be little doubt but that the
simplest form of stringed instrument (played with
a bow) was conceived from the idea of a stretched
string fixed at two *points*, vibration being excited
by means of a jagged stick. The earliest known
instrument of this species, according to M. Fétis (a
great historical writer on the subject) is the ravanastron, stated to have been invented by an ancient
King of Ceylon, called Ravana, some five or six
thousand years ago. It consisted of a cylinder of

sycamore wood, hollowed out from one end to the
other. " This cylinder is about 4¾ inches long, and
has a diameter of 2 inches. Over one end is
stretched a piece of boa skin, with large scales,
which forms the belly or sound-board. The cylinder
is crossed from side to side—at one-third of its
length, next the sound-board—by a rod or shank
of deal, which serves as a neck, of the length of 22
inches, rounded on its under part, but flat on the top,
and slightly inclined backwards. The head of this
neck is pierced with two holes for the pegs, half an
inch in diameter; not in the side, but in the plane
of the sound-board. Two large pegs, 4 inches in
length, shaped hexagonally at the top, and rounded
at the ends which go into the holes, serve to tighten
two strings made of the intestines of the gazelle,
which are fixed to a strap of serpent skin attached
to the lower extremity of the rod or shank. A little
bridge ¾ of an inch long, cut sloping on the top,
but flat on the part which rests on the sound-board,
and worked out rectangularly in this part, so as
to form two separate feet, supports the strings.
As to the bow, it is formed of a small bamboo, of

which the upper portion is slightly curved, and the lower (nearly) straight. A hole is made in the head of the bow, at the first knot, for fixing a hank of hair, which is strained and fixed at the other end, by binding a very flexible rush string twenty times round it."

Such is this most primitive bow instrument, slight modifications of which still exist in Eastern countries. The Chinese and Japanese fiddles one often sees now in music-shops are not at all unlike the ancient ravanastron. That India appears to have given birth to bow instruments, and to have made them known to other parts of Asia, Egypt and afterwards to Europe, no conjecture is needed, for the instruments themselves exist, and still preserve the characteristics of their native originality.

We will now pass over a few thousand years during which time stringed instruments of great variety and of every conceivable shape had been invented and improved upon in different countries of the world, their gradual development (brought about, no doubt, more by circumstances existing at various periods than by any real aim towards artistic achievement) giving birth to the various families of stringed instruments in use at the present day, e.g., the violin family, the harp, guitar, mandoline and pianoforte.

❊   ❊   ❊   ❊   ❊   ❊

In tracing the progress of the violin (which the author will endeavour to do in connection with its music and performers) it is necessary to content ourselves with a more definite standpoint, therefore, we will commence with a period when the viol or fiddle family came upon the scene, the immediate precursor of the violin; the viol, in fact, is not inaptly termed the grandfather of the violin.

The great distinctive feature between a viol and the present violin family, is that instead of F sound-holes, viols had C holes. Some had sound-holes in the shape of what are known as " flaming sword " holes. They carried five or six strings, sometimes more, and the finger-board was mounted with frets, for (as was then thought) the more certain means of stopping the notes in perfect tune, an idea which, to modern violinists, involves an absurdity.

Viols are known to have been in use as early as

the fifteenth century (some writers go back to the
thirteenth, but these early ones partook more of the
nature and shape of the guitar than of the subsequent viol). The viol continued in use up to the beginning of the reign of Charles I, and was one of the
most popular instruments in its time. There were
generally four in use, viz., treble, alto, tenor and bass,
and occupied in some respects the position now held
by our violin, tenor, 'cello and double bass. To an
ordinary observer there is little difference in appearance between the shape of a treble viol and the
earliest violin, so that a considerable latitude of
doubt may be allowed to exist as to the finality of
the former and the adoption of the latter; but certain it is that the violin of the time became to be
appreciated to such an extraordinary degree, that
the principal viol and lute makers towards the end
of the sixteenth century set about making violins in
the place of viols. Whether the idea of this change
was dictated by the caprice of novelty, or whether
any special demand arose for an instrument of more
extended compass by reason of the advancement
made in the musical compositions of the time, it is

difficult to determine with certainty. It is signifi-
cant, however, that at this period of the advancement of the violin, the musical influence of Tallis
(the founder of English church music), and of Bird,
his illustrious pupil, was manifesting itself throughout this country, and in Italy the music of Palestrina
exercised a similar influence.

In the year 1662 appeared the first work printed
in England containing any reference to the violin.
It was written by one John Playford, and is entitled
" A Brief Introduction to the Skill of Musick,"
wherein is the following relating to the violin :

" The treble violin is a cheerful and sprightly
instrument, and much practised of late, some by
book, and some without; which of these two is the
best way, may easily be resolved. First, to learn
to play by rote or ear, without book, is the way never
to play more than what he can guess by seeing and
hearing another play, which may soon be forgotten,
but, on the contrary, he which learns and practices
by book, according to the rules of musick, fails not
after he comes to be perfect under these rules, which
guide him to play more than ever he was taught

or heard, and also to play his part in concert, the
which the other will never be capable of, unless he
hath this usual guide.

"These rules of music are in a plain method, as
it shows in the first six chapters of this book, the
which being perfectly understood, viz., the notes of
the scale or gamut, which directs the places of all
notes, flat and sharp, by which are pricked all les-
sons and tunes on the five lines, thus distinguishing
of the several parts by their cliffs, as the treble,
tenor, and basse. Lastly, the names of the notes,
their quantities, proportions, and rests, according to
the rule of keeping time, etc. There then remains
two things to be instructed in, how the violin is
strung and tuned, and secondly, to give you direc-
tions for the stopping the several notes, both flat
and sharp, in their right places. Then, first observe
that this cannot be expressed in words unless on
the neck or finger-board of the violin there be set
five or six frets, as is on the viol. This, though it
be not usual, yet it is the best and easiest way for
a beginner, for by it he has a certain rule to
direct him to stop all his notes in exact tune, which

those that do learn without seldom attain so good
an ear to stop all notes in perfect tune. Therefore,
for the better understanding of these following examples, I shall assign to those six frets on the
finger-board of your violin six letters of the alpha-
bet in their order" (here follow examples), after
which he says :

"These few rules (and the help of an able master
to instruct thee in the true fingering, and the several
graces and flourishes that are necessary to be learnt
by such as desire to be exquisite hereon), will in a
short time make thee an able proficient."

These quaint instructions would hardly suffice to
meet the requirements of modern violin playing, but
it is interesting to observe the rules and precepts
laid down for the student's guidance over two hun-
dred years ago. Observe also the recommendation
of frets for accuracy in stopping the notes.

The viol, however, was not destined to die a sud-
den death, at any rate, in this country. The soft
wailing tone of the viol still found many admirers,
principally amongst amateurs, who regarded the
violin in the nature of an interloper. Their cause

too was vindicated by one Thomas Mace, who, curious to relate, was born in the same year as John Playford (1613). This worthy lived in Cambridge, and in 1676 published a work entitled "Musick's Monument, cr a Remembrancer of the best practical music both Divine and Civil that has ever been known to be in the world," certainly a most ambi-tious title and one that does not in the least suffer on its comparison with the precepts contained in the book. He was one of the clerks of Trinity College, Cambridge, and seemed to have acquired consider-able knowledge of matters musical. Under whom he was educated, or by what means he became pos-sessed of so much skill as to be able to furnish mat-ter for the above work, he has nowhere informed us. We may collect from it that he was enthusiastically fond of music, and of a devout and serious disposi-tion, though cheerful and good humoured.

His knowledge of music seems to have been con-fined to the practice of the lute (his favourite in-strument) and the viol. The third part of this work is devoted chiefly to the viol, and in this he cen-sures the abuse of music in the number of bass and

treble instruments in the concerts of his time, in
which he says, it was not unusual to have but one
small weak-sounding bass viol to two or three
"scoulding violins." This disproportion he seeks to
remedy by the observance of the following instructions. He says :

"Your best provision (and most compleat) will be
a good chest of viols six in number, viz., 2 basses,
2 tenors, and 2 trebles. All truly and proportion-
ably suited. Of such, there are no better in the
world than those of Aldred, Jay, Smith (yet the
highest in esteem are), Bolles and Ross (one bass of
Bolles I have known valued at £100).

"These were old, but we have now very excellent
good workmen who (no doubt) can work as well as
those if they be so well paid for their work as they
were, yet we chiefly value old instruments before
new, for by experience they are found to be far the
best. The reason for which I can no further dive
into than to say, I apprehend that by extream age
the wood (and those other adjuncts) glew, parch-
ment, paper, lynings of cloath (as some use), but
above all the vernish. These are all so very much

(by time) dryed. Linefied, made gentle, rarified, or (to say better even) agefied, so that that stiffness, stubbornness, or clunginess, which is natural to such bodies are so debilitated and made plyable, that the pores of the wood have a more and free liberty to move, stir, or secretly vibrate, by which means the air (which is the life of all things both animate and inanimate), has a more free and easy recourse to pass and repass, and whether I have hit upon the right cause I know not, but sure I am that age adds goodness to instruments, therefore they have the advantage of all our late workmen.

"Now suppose you cannot procure an entire chest of viols suitable, etc. Then thus. Endeavour to pick up (here or there) so many excellent good odd ones as near suiting as you can (every way), viz., both for shape, wood, colour, etc., but especially for size. And to be exact in that take this certain rule, viz., let your bass be larger, then your trebles must be just as short again in the string, viz., from bridge to nut, as are your basses, because they should stand 8 notes higher than the basses. Therefore, as short again (for the middle of every string is an 8th) the

tenors (in the string) just so long as from the bridge
to F fret because they stand a 4th higher.

" Let this suffice to put you into a complete order
for viols."

We have given the above quotation *in extenso*
without breaking in with any comment, in order that
the student may better understand the peculiar
phraseology used by this ancient authority. The student will observe that old instruments were equally
valued in those days as in these, and this too was at
a period anterior to the fame of the great Stradivarius, whose grand period commenced with the
opening of the eighteenth century.*

There appears to be a general consensus of
opinion favouring the theory that Gaspar da Salo,

* That Cremona instruments were held in high estimation
during the reign of Charles II, is proved by the following
entry in the Enrolments of the Audit Office, 1662, vol. vi :
" These are to require you to pay, or cause to be paid to John
Bannister, one of his Majesties musicians in ordinary, the
some of fourty poundes for two cremona violins, by him
bought and delivered for his Majesties service as may appear
by the bill annexed, and also tenn pounds for strings for two
years, ending 24th June, 1662. And this shall be your war-
rant, etc."

the founder of the Brescian school of violin makers, who probably worked from 1560 to 1610, was the first to make violins in their present shape. Be this as it may, no mention is made of any of his instruments having found their way into this country at this period, nor is he mentioned in any way in connection with the adoption of the violin in this country, the probability is that our own viol and lute makers commenced a school of their own, although nothing definite seems to be known as to who they were. One thing, however, seems certain, the early English violin makers were far behind the Italians in point of workmanship. The English model was large and clumsy, while that of Italy left hardly any room for improvement.

* * * * *

The derivation of the word fiddle* appears to be wrapt in obscurity, and must in no way be taken as coeval with the term violin. According to Strutt, the antiquary (who wrote a very interesting work last century on the sports and pastimes of the early Eng-

* In early English times the word "crowd" was often used instead of fiddle.

lish), the name of fiddler was applied to the minstrels
or itinerant musicians of the fourteenth century.
Chaucer, in his " Canterbury Tales," mentions the term
in connection with " The Clerke of Oxenforde."

> For him was lever han at his beddes head
> A Twenty Bokys clothyd in blacke or rede
> Of Aristotel and hys philosophie
> Than robys riche or fidel or sautrie.

In the " Vision of Pierce the Ploughman," we read
" not to fare as a Fydeler or a Frier to seke Feastes."

It would appear that as time went on, these wandering minstrels or fiddlers sunk very much in
popular estimation, and were held in very low esteem, so much so, that in the reign of Elizabeth was
passed an Act entitled " An Act for the punishment
of rogues, vagabonds, and sturdy beggars,"* and
amongst the malefactors amenable under this Act
were included " ' Wandering Minstrels ' (other than
players of interludes belonging to any Barron of
the realm, or any other honourable personage of
greater degree if authorised to play under the hand
and seal of arms of such Baron, or personage ") the

* This Act was repealed by 12 Ann Stat. 2, C. 23.

penalty being "such pain and punishment as by this Act is in that behalf appointed."

We hear of the itinerant musician again in an ordinance from Oliver Cromwell dated 1656, during his protectorship, which prohibited "all persons commonly called fidlers or minstrels" from "playing, fidling and making music in any inn, alehouse or tavern," and also from "proffering themselves, or desiring or intreating any one to hear them play or make music in the places aforesaid."

The great moralist, Owen Feltham, in his "Resolves," 1631, also touches upon the subject. Under his remarks on music we read: "It is a kind of disparagement to bee a cunning fiddler. It argues his neglect of better employment and that he hath spent much time upon a thing unnecessarie. Hence it hath been counted ill for great ones to sing and play like an arted musician, Philip asked Alexander if hee was not ashamed that he 'sang so artfully.'" In the "Westminster Magazine" for February, 1775, is an article entitled "Fiddling Defended," as follows:

"Some people are unreasonably severe against Fiddlers, but surely there is no absurdity in attracting the eyes of the fair in displaying a white hand, a ring, a ruffle, or sleeve to advantage. Who can blame the performer who is successful enough to fiddle himself into a good fortune? Whatever the rigid and austere may think, the approbation of the ladies is no small spur to a proficiency in music as well as in many other sciences. It is highly probable that Achilles (though the blind bard is silent upon this head) would not have strummed his harp with so much glee if the ears of Deidamia and Brifeis had not been tickled by it.—A FIDDLER."

Peacham, in his description of a "Compleat Gentleman," published 1634, addresses his readers thus : "I desire no more in you than to sing your part sure and at first sight, and withall to play the same upon your violl or the exercise of the lute privately to yourselfe"—and in another place he observes : "King Henry the eighth could not onely sing his part sure but of himselfe compose a service of foure five and sixe parts"—and we are told that Queen Elizabeth was a tolerable performer on the virginals (the precursor of the pianoforte) and also the violin.

3

The next source from which any historic information concerning the fiddle is obtained is from the writings of one Anthony Wood, of Oxford, who, although not a professional player, was an enthusiastic amateur whose opinion was not to be despised.

This worthy in his life written by himself in the year 1654 gives an amusing account of a musical escapade which it may not be out of place here to repeat, as the work is rather scarce and difficult of access. It throws an interesting light on the state of music at that period. He says:

"Having by this time got some musical acquaintance, a frolick by all meanes must be taken by us; and what should it be, but to disguise ourselves in poore habits, and like contry fidlers scrape for our livings? Faringdon Fair this yeare was the place designed to go to: And all of us (five in number) lodging in a house in the Middle Rew in Magd. parish,—belonging to one Gregory a Chandler, wee sate out very early the next morning, and calling first on Mr. Th. Latton's house at Kingston Baképuze, wee bid him good morrow by 2 or 3 tunes. He came in the hall among us, listened to our musick, gave us money, and ordered drink to (be) carried to us. After wee had done with him, wee retired to the In standing on the road going to Farringdon, dined there, and after dinner wee were entertain'd by some of the neighbours, who danc'd (as I remember) on the Green, gave us some money and victualls, and I think wee returned very late that evening to Oxon. The names of those in this exploit were, myself and Will Bull before mentioned, who played on the Violins, Edm. Gregorie, B.A., and gent. com. of Mert. Coll. who play'd on the bass viol, John Nap of Trinity on the citerne, and George Mason, of the said Coll. on another wyer instrument, but could do nothing. Soon after we took a voyage northward, called at Hampton Poyle, played at Mr. Wests' house, had some money, but more drink. Afterwards we went (I think) to Kidlington, got something there, returned in the evening, and certain soldiers overtaking us, they by force, made us play in the open field, and then left us without giving a penny.

"Most of my companions would afterwards glory in this, but I was ashamed, and could never endure to hear of it."

He goes on to relate that by 1656 he "had a genuine skill in musick, and frequented the weekly meetings of musitians in the house of Will Ellis, late
Organist of St. Johns Coll., situated and being in a
house, opposite to that place whereon the Theatre
was built." Here he gives a list of the company
who met and performed their parts on lutes and
viols. The music masters were: "Will Ellis,
Batchelor of Musick, and owner of the house, who
always played his part either on the organ or virginal:—Dr. John Wilson, the public professor, the
best at the lute in all England. He sometimes
play'd on the lute, but mostly presided (directed)
the consort.—Curteys, a lutenist, lately ejected from
some choire or cathedral church. Thomas Jackson,
a bass violist. . . . Ed. Low, Organist lately of
Christ Church. He play'd only on the organ; so
when he played on that instrument Mr. Ellis would
take up the counter-tenor viol, if any person were
wanting to perform that part. Gervace Littleton
. . . . a violist; he was afterwards a singing man of
St. Johns Coll. Will Glexney, who had belonged to
a choire before the warr . . . . he played well upon

the bass-viol, and sometimes sung his part . . . .
Proctor, a young man and a new comer. John
Parker, one of the university musitians. But Mr.
Low, a proud man, could not endure any common
musitians to come to the meeting, much less to play
among them. Of this kind I must rank John Hasel-
wood, an apothecary, a starch'd formal clister-pipe,
who usually played on the bass-viol, and sometimes
on the counter-tenor. He was very conceited of his
skill (though he had but little of it) and therefore
would be ever and anon ready to take up a viol
before his betters, which being observed by all, they
usually called him 'Handlewood.' The rest were
but beginners.

"Proctor died soon after this time, he had been
bred up for Mr. John Jenkyns, the mirrour and wonder of his age for musick, was excellent for the
lyra-viol, and division-viol, good at the treble-viol,
and treble-violin, and all comprehended in a man of
three or four and twenty years of age. He was much
admired at the meetings, and exceedingly pitied by
all the facultie for his loss."

"A. W. was now advised to entertain one Will

James, a dancing master, to instruct him on the violin, who by some was accounted excellent on that instrument, and the rather, because it was said that he had obtained his knowledge in dancing and musick in France. He spent, in all, half a yeare with him, and gained some improvement from him; yet at length he found him not a compleat master of his facultie, as Griffith and Parker were not; and, to say the truth, there was no complete master in Oxon for that instrument, because it *had not hitherto been used in consort* among gentlemen, only by common musitians, who played but two parts. The gentle men in private meetings, which A. W. frequented, played three, four, and five parts with viols, as treble-viol, tenor, counter tenor, and bass, with an Organ, virginal or harpsicon joyn'd with them; and they esteemed a violin to be an instrument only belonging to a *common fiddler*, and could not endure that it should come among them, for feare of making their meetings to be vaine and fiddling. But before the restoration of King Charles II, and especially after, viols began to be out of fashion, and only violins used, as treble-violin, tenor, and bass violin; and the King, according to the French mode, would have 24 violins playing before him while he was at meales, as being more airie and brisk than viols."

Under the year 1658 he informs us that: " Tho. Baltzar, a Lubecker borne, and the most famous artist for the violin that the world had yet produced, was now in Oxon.   And this day (July 24th), A. W. was with him and Mr. Ed. Low at the Meeting house of Will Ellis.   A. W. did then and there, to his very great astonishment, heare him play on the violin.   He then saw him run up his fingers to the end of the finger-board of the violin, and run them back insensibly, and all in alacrity and in very good tune, which he nor any in England saw the like before.   A. W. entertained him and Mr. Low with what the house could then afford, and afterwards he invited them to the tavern; but they being engag'd to goe to other company, he could no more heare him play or see him play at that time.   Afterwards he came to one of the weekly meetings, at Mr. Ellis's House, and he played to the wonder of all the auditory; and exercising his fingers and instrument several wayes to the utmost of his power. Wilson, thereupon, the public professor (the greatest judge of musick that ever was) did, after his humoursome way stoope downe to Baltzar's feet to see whether he had a huff (hoof) on, that is to say, to see whether he was a devil or not, because he acted beyond the parts of man."

"About this time it was, that Dr. John Wilkins, warden of Wadham Coll., the greatest curioso of his time, invited him and some of the musitians to his lodgings in that Coll. purposely to have a consort, and to see and heare him play. The instruments and books were carried thither, but none could be persuaded there to play against him in consort on the violin.

"At length the company perceiving A. W. standing behind in a corner, neare the dore, they haled him in among them, and play, forsooth he must, against him. Whereupon he being not able to avoid it, took up a violin and behaved himself as poor Troylus did against Achilles. He was abashed at it, yet honour he got by playing with and against such a grand master as Baltzar was."

" Mr. Davis Mell was accounted hitherto the best for the violin in England, as I have before told you, but after Baltzar came into England, and showed his most wonderful parts on that instrument, Mell was not so admired, yet he played sweeter, was a well bred gentleman, and not given to excessive drinking as Baltzar was."

✻   ✻   ✻   ✻   ✻

Baltzar occupies a twofold prominence, he was one of the earliest German performers, and the first to give any real impetus towards the popularity of the violin in this country. He is also stated to have been the first to introduce the practice of "shifting."

✻   ✻   ✻

During the reign of Charles I, and also during the Cromwellian usurpation, music was practically at a standstill. Instrumental music in churches was prohibited, and the theatres were soon after shut up. Indeed, as a previous historian of the art has observed, "nothing but syllabic· and unisonous psalmody was authorised or even permitted in the Church. Organs were taken down; organists and choirmen reduced to beggary, and the art of music,

and indeed all arts but those of killing, canting,
and hypocracy, discountenanced, if not prescribed.
The only demand made for the fiddle was in the
performance of low class music as an accompaniment to the bacchanalian orgies, in favour during
this profligate period."

However, with the restoration of Charles II, came
the restoration of music in this country. The musical taste of this monarch having been formed in
France during his sojourn there, he was naturally
anxious to introduce the French style into this country, and as we have seen from the writings of
A. Wood, he emulated the French King, Louis XIV,
by employing a band of twenty-four violins. From
this period, and with this impetus, the epoch of
violin playing in England may be said to date.

The leader of this band of twenty-four violins was
Baltzar; he was succeeded by John Banister, who
was really the first English violinist of any note.

Pepys, in his Diary, under date February 20,
1667, says: "They talk how the King's violin Banister is made. That a Frenchman (Louis Grabu) is
come to be chief of some part of the King's music."

It is worthy of notice that Banister was sent abroad by Charles II in order to study music and acquire the French taste, and so fit himself for the leadership of the King's band, which post, however, he soon lost for asserting in the King's hearing that the English violinists were superior to those of France, which probably accounts for the note made by Pepys in his Diary.

Banister must have been a very enthusiastic musician, for he was the first who publicly advertised concerts in this country.

The following advertisement is extracted from the "London Gazette," under date Monday, December 30, 1672.

"These are to give notice, that at Mr. John Bannister's House (now called the Music School) over against the George Tavern in White Fryers, this present Monday, will be musick performed by excellent Masters, beginning precisely at 4 of the Clock in the afternoon, and every afternoon, for the future precisely at the same hour."

   ❄   ❄   ❄   ❄   ❄   ❄

We have now arrived at the close of the seventeenth century, by which time the supremacy of the violin was established not only in England, but in all countries where culture and the fine arts march hand in hand.

*　　*　　*　　*　　*　　*

Before bringing this notice to a close, let us glance briefly at the artistic activity prevailing during the early part of the eighteenth century.

In his workshop at Cremona would be found the great violin maker, Antonius Stradivarius, producing those inimitable instruments which have rendered him so famous. We find Corelli at the head of the first school of violinists at Rome (of which he was the founder), turning out pupils destined to shed lustre into whatever country they carried their art, and writing those immortal sonatas, that will ever retain their high character as examples of tonal purity, and with Boccherini, laying the foundation of chamber music.

In 1714 the arrival in England of Geminiani and Veracini, the great Italian violinists, contributed to make the violin more popular as well as to advance the practice of execution. They also supplied the performers on that instrument with compositions far superior to any they had possessed prior to their arrival.

The establishment of Italian opera in England served to raise up a host of violinists, who were not slow in availing themselves of the facilities afforded them for studying under the great Italian masters continually visiting this country. The result has been, that England at the present day is able to point with pride to some of the most notable performers on the violin, as belonging to her ranks.

II.—ITALY,

In musical execution, the early schools of Italy showed a marked superiority over the rest of Europe, particularly with regard to the violin.

Corelli, who was born in 1653, was the first to establish a new school in instrumental composition, distinguished from that which preceded it by a graceful, rhythmical and natural manner of writing. He was the first composer who brought the violin into repute; and his originality, facility and delicacy of style, greatly contributed to the popularity of the violin. He was founder of the Roman, or what may now be called the ancient school of violinists, and obtained the proud title of " Princeps Musicorum." After the publication of Corelli's works, there was scarcely a town in Italy where the

violin was not cultivated and in which some distinguished performer on that instrument did not
reside. Most of his contemporaries formed themselves on his model—as Albioni, of Venice, Torelli,
of Verona, Valentini (whose works were published
in Holland), and Marietto, who was a Neapolitan
violinist attached to the household of the Duke of
Orleans.

Tartini, born 1692, the most celebrated performer
on the violin of his day, formed all his scholars on
the solos of Corelli.* He was the first who observed
the phenomenon of the third sound, which he did in
the year 1714, at Venice. This is the resonance of a
third note when the two upper notes of a chord are
sounded; and may be distinctly heard if a series of
consecutive thirds are played on the violin, they
being perfectly in tune.

*　　*　　*　　*

Let us now briefly notice the two great Italian

* James Sherard, an Englishman, also composed several
sonatas, so nearly equal to Corelli's, and resembling them
so perfectly in style, that they might have been taken for
that composer's.

schools of violin makers, which, up to the end of the seventeenth century, had been called into existence.

The first was the Brescian school, the founder of which was Gasparo da Salo. This maker, as we have mentioned elsewhere, was the first to introduce the violin in its present size and shape. The next representative of this school was John Paul Maggini, who worked from 1600 to 1640. Other makers there were, viz., Mariani, Buddiani, Ambrosi, Bente, Pietro Sancto Maggini (son of J. P. Maggini), but they call for no special comment.

The next great school was the Cremonese, founded by Andreas Amati, who was succeeded by his sons, Antony and Hieronymus Amati, and they worked together for some time. The most noted of this family was Nicolas Amati (born 1596, died 1684). The Cremonese renown for violin making, however, attained its climax in the productions of Antony Stradivarius (1644-1737) and Joseph Guarnerius (1683-1745). The various lesser lights who worked in these two schools will be duly noticed in the biographical portion of this work.

✧   ✧   ✳   ✳   ✳

The music of this period falls next to be noticed.
Mr. Charles Reade, in his able articles on Cremona
fiddles, which appeared in the August numbers of
the "Pall Mall Gazette" for 1872, states, "Man in-
vents only to supply a want." This observation is
peculiarly applicable to the violin; for we find that
with the advancement of musical composition came
the desire to attain greater perfection in the art of
violin making. This is illustrated by the fact that
the performance of modern music would be next to
impossible on one of the old violins, by reason of
the then shortness of the neck; hence arises the
necessity for refitting old violins with longer necks,
thus giving the performer greater command over the
high notes, and adding largely to the strength of
the instrument.

The use of the violin in the orchestra began to
receive recognition with the dawn of the seventeenth
century. Monteverde, in his opera of "Orfeo,"
printed in 1615, scores for "two little French violins" (*piccoli violini alla Francese*).

Without referring to the periods anterior to the
seventeenth century, concerning which we have little

or no information, we know that during the first two generations of that century, music in Italy was mostly in the madrigal style. The capabilities of instrumental music, apart from the voice, however, were soon discovered, and composers entered gladly upon a new and wide field of musical effort. The compositions were usually comprehended under the names of studies, fantasias, capricci, sonatas, concertos and other pieces in various styles.

Corelli has been accredited with fixing the form of the sonata, and Torelli, his contemporary, with inventing the concerto.

When dramatic music began to prevail under Corelli, it was scientific and rather dry, Geminiani first enriched it by expression; but it was under Tartini that it attained the highest degree of expression, both as to composition and execution. Soon after this period the concerto was greatly improved in the hands of Jarnowick and Mestrino, both of whom were still surpassed by Viotti, who gave to this style the character which seems so peculiarly its own and brought it to a degree of perfection which it seems incapable of exceeding.

These remarks apply equally to solo as to con-
certed music: by which term we understand music
for several voices or instruments, the parts of which
do not stand in the relation of solo and accompani-
ments, but are of nearly equal importance; equally
obbligato, either because each of them has its appro-
priate part, or because each takes up the strain
successively, the others alternately becoming accom-
paniments. This method is practically alike in the
duet, the trio, the quartet, the quintet, and other
pieces where each instrument has its separate part.

Boccherini was the first who, in 1768, gave to these
forms a fixed character. After him came Fiorillo,
Giardini, Pugnani, and lastly, Viotti.

Such was the style of music, so far as the violin
is concerned, from the time of Corelli to the commencement of this century.

Although Italy has since had to yield the palm
for instrumental music to other countries, we must
not overlook the fact that for generations she held
undisputed sway in the realm of music; both as
regards composers and performers.

III.—FRANCE.

WE will now direct our attention to France.

Towards the latter end of the sixteenth century the lute was a very favourite and general instrument. About the year 1577 the violin was introduced by Baltazarini, a then celebrated performer, who was sent at the head of a band of performers by Marshal Brissac to Catherine de Medicis, and was appointed valet de chambre to the Princess. Beyond this little appears to be known of him.

We have elsewhere had occasion to refer to the band of twenty-four violins of Louis XIV. The leader of this band was a Florentine named Lully, who was instrumental in introducing the Italian music into France, thus giving to that country a new musical existence. The high standard then prevailing in

Italy, he, however, failed to maintain, but be this as
it may, the French seemed to have acquired a kind
of distinctive reputation as performers, for M.
Choron says : " With respect to the style in which the
French have real and undisputed merit, and, indeed,
in many respects have a marked superiority, is the instrumental in general, and especially that of the violin. . . . The excellence of the twenty-four violins of
Louis XIV formed by Lully and of other violinists,
was highly spoken of so far back as the seventeenth
century," and he adds, " I do not, however, know how
to reconcile these facts with the following remark of
Corette* in the preface to his " Method of Accompaniment," published at Paris about the year 1750.
'At the commencement of this century' (says
Corette) 'music was very dull and slow,' etc. . . .
When Corelli's sonatas were first brought from
Rome (about 1715), nobody in Paris could play
them. The Duke of Orleans, then Regent, being a
great amateur of music, and wishing to hear them,
was obliged to have them *sung* by three voices. The

* Michael Corette was an organist in Paris in 1738. He
wrote several treatises on music.

violinists then begun to study them, and, at the expiration of some years, three were found who could
play them. Baptiste, one of these, went to Rome to
study them under Corelli himself," and M. Choron
continuing, says : " Be this as it may, since that
period, instrumental music has been studied with
ardour by the French, and they have made astonishing progress in it. France has now an excellent
school for the violin, founded upon that of Italy."

It seems rather astonishing to believe that singers
could be found to sing that which took a violinist
years of practice to perform, especially in view
of the fact that France at that period almost
neglected the vocal art, and we must regard Corette's
criticism as somewhat biased, notwithstanding he
was " a furious partisan of the French school of
music."

No doubt the French had to supply their reper-
toires of chamber music (when they required it)
from the Italian composers, the music of France in
Lully's time being mostly composed for the lyric
drama, which was then greatly in vogue.

The first to call into existence a French school

was Jean Marie Leclair, who received his instructions from Somis, an Italian.   He does not, however, appear to have formed any great performers,
owing, probably, to the European fame of the great
Italian masters. According to one historian the real
founder of the French school was Pierre Gavinies,
born at Bordeaux in 1726. Be this so or not, he
certainly produced some fine masters. Indeed, during the eighteenth century, France was productive
of the finest violinists that had been heard. We have
only to mention such names as Lahousaye, Barthélé-
mon, Rode, Kreutzer, Lafont, Baillot, Habeneck and
De Beriot, in proof of this assertion.

*　*　*　*　*　*

The early records of violin making in France, like
those of other countries, seem buried in obscurity.
Its literature offers but scant information of a reliable character, and we are therefore compelled to
make the most of such evidence as is afforded by the
slender testimony of paintings and ecclesiastical
monuments.

We are told that Baltazarini was the first to introduce the violin (or rather the performance of it) into

France, in the year 1577, so that it is safe to assume no maker of any note existed anterior to this period. One authority tells us that, in the year 1566, the name of Tywersus of Nancy appears as a lute and violin maker, and is reported to have assisted Andreas Amati to finish certain instruments made for the chapel of Charles IX. Soon after this period several names of makers are recorded, but little seems to be known of them, or of their work.

Excellence in violin making seems to have commenced with the middle of the eighteenth century, when the name of Nicholas Lupot appears on the scene as the founder of the French school. Before he died, however, in 1824, France had given birth to John Baptiste Vuillaume, in whose hands the construction of violins attained the utmost perfection. His instruments are much admired and often realise large sums of money. Many makers of great merit have since cropped up, which has had the effect of establishing France as the greatest producer of the instrument, the subject of these pages.

IV.—GERMANY.

LET us now direct our spirit of inquiry into Germany, that land of music and musicians. This country, notwithstanding its present musical position appears to have been somewhat behind the times in regard to the production of any early violin performers of note, and affords the names of fewer musicians than almost any other country during the sixteenth century, if we except Spain. An explanation of this seems to be afforded by the fact of the wars, which devastated Germany during the latter part of the sixteenth and beginning of the seventeenth centuries, and particularly the terrible Thirty Years' war, during which five great armies overran that unhappy country, carrying desolation and havoc in every part of it. These wars destroyed the arts, which can only flourish in the bosom of peace and happiness. It is certain that at this period the school of Germany was greatly inferior to that of Italy; it even appears that the French school began before the German to emerge from obscurity. Reason is wanting to account for the German lack of early performers, but we feel constrained to borrow the following words from Dubourg. He says : " We may observe, that, although derived originally, like all others, from that of Italy, and contracting no inconsiderable obligations to it in its progress, it has been, on the whole, much less indebted to the Italians for resources and support, than the school either of France or England."

Although the early German performers were inferior as soloists to those of Italy or France, they were certainly able to hold their own as orchestral players. Be this as it may, they have certainly, in modern times, produced some of the finest violinists the world has seen; the music too, has long since supplanted that of Italy.

Thomas Baltzar, born at Lubec about 1630, was esteemed the finest violin performer of his time; but

he came to England as we have seen in 1658, and
helped to rescue the violin from the low estimation
in which it was then held, an honour, however, he
only lived five years to enjoy.

It was not until the early part of the eighteenth
century that any attempts were made to establish a
German violin school. Amongst the first to diffuse
any artistic influence may be mentioned Francis
Benda, 1709-86, and John Stamitz, 1719-61, but the
honour of founding a distinct school must be
awarded to Leopold Mozart (father of the great
W. A. Mozart) and after him came William Cramer,
who ultimately came to England; these were followed by J. Salomon and Kiesewetter.

Louis Spohr, born 1784, may rightly be termed
the founder of the modern German school, he was
both a performer and composer of the highest order.
The names of Guhr, Mayseder and Molique are also
well known as performers of great merit.

*   *   *   *   *   *

Violin making in Germany commenced with the
name of Jacobus Stainer, born at Hall, near Absam,
in the Tyrol, 1621, died 1683. It has been said,

though without authority, that he was an apprentice of Nicholas Amati, a statement which would gain little credence on comparing the instruments of each of these makers.

The next makers in succession are the Klotz family (six in number), 1670-1741. Other makers will be found in the biographical section.

PART II.

BIOGRAPHICAL.

VIOLIN MAKERS OF THE OLD SCHOOLS.

I.—ITALIAN.

ALBANI, MATTHIAS, born at Botzen in the Tyrol, 1621, died there 1673. He adopted the Stainer model, and produced some very fine instruments.

> **MA ttio A lban fecit Bolzan . 17**

ALBANI, MATTHIAS, son and pupil of the foregoing. He afterwards went to Cremona to study the art in the Amati school, and afterwards adopted that model with great success.

> **MATTHIAS Albanus mefecit, Bulfani in Tyroli. 1706**

AMATI, ANDREAS, born about 1520, died about 1580. Founder of the Cremonese school. It is conjectured that he was a pupil of Gasparo da Salo. He adopted rather a small model, built rather high in the centre. Backs cut on the layers, deep golden varnish, and perfect finish, are the chief characteristics of this maker.

The tone is sweet and sympathetic, but lacks brilliancy; they are therefore valued more on account of their historical associations than as a musical medium.

AMATI, ANTONIUS and **AMATI, HIERONYMUS,** flourished 1570-1635. These two were sons of Andreas. They worked together it is presumed for some time, and produced many instruments of great beauty. The wood was well chosen and handsomely figured. The model selected was not quite so high as that adopted by the father. The *f* holes are of beautiful shape, and the backs are cut variously in the whole or slab. The purfling, which is of exquisite quality, is inserted with the utmost skill. The tone of the instruments made by this ancient firm is sweet and pure, but is deficient in power.

Antonius, & Hieronym. Fr. Amati
Cremonen. Andrex fil. F. 16

Antonius, & Hieronimus Fr.
Amati Cremonen, AndrexF. 16

AMATI, NICOLAS, born 1596, died 1684. He was the son of Hieronymus, and the best artist of his family. His first efforts were simply copies of the firm last mentioned. His most celebrated fiddles are known as " Grand Amati's." He somewhat flattened the model of his father, and continued the arching nearer the sides, where it forms a sinking in round the edges. The *f* holes are exquisitely cut, and the corners are long and strongly pronounced. The wood chosen for the bellies has a fine even grain, and the backs are beautifully marked. The varnish used by Nicolas was deeper and richer than that used by the other members of the family.

The following is a facsimile of an authentic ticket of this great maker.

Nicolaus Amatus Cremonen. Hieronymi
Fil. ac Antonij Nepos Fecit. 1677

BERGONZI, CARLO, Cremona, flourished
1718-47. This maker was the best pupil of Stradivarius. He at first copied his great master, but subsequently started a model of his own; rather broad
and heavy, and flat arching. The scroll is strongly
pronounced and finely cut. The *f* holes, which are
unusually long, are placed low in the body, and very
near the purfling. The wood is carefully selected
and the general workmanship is of superior finish;
only equalled by Nicolas Amati or Stradivarius.
The varnish used by Bergonzi was reddish brown,
rather thickly applied.

Anno 1733 Carlo Bergonzi
fece in Cremona.

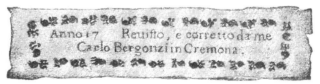

Anno 17   Reuifto, e corretto da me
Carlo Bergonzi in Cremona.

BERGONZI, MICHAEL ANGELO, Cre-
mona, 1720-60, son of Carlo, made good instruments,
but they certainly suffer on comparison with those of
his father. This maker had two sons called respectively Nicolaus, and Zosimo, who followed the same
calling from 1739-65.

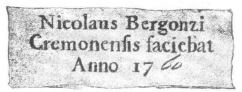

Nicolaus Bergonzi
Cremonenfis faciebat
Anno 17 66

Fatto da me Zolimo Bergonzi
l'anno 17   Cremona

CAPPA, GIOFREDO, an early maker who
worked in Cremona about 1590 to 1640. He was a
pupil of Hieronymus and Antonius Amati, when
those brothers were in partnership. In 1640 he proceeded to Piedmont and founded the school of
Saluzzio, and formed there many good pupils.
Cappa succeeded best in the manufacture of violoncellos.

IOFREDVS CAPPA FECIT
SALVTVS ANNO 1630

GAGLIANO, ALLESSANDRO, born about
1640, died at Naples in 1725. He is said to have
commenced operation in Cremona, working under
Stradivarius. His instruments are flat in model,
rather large, and generally of fairly good tone
throughout. Varnish light yellow. The badly cut
scrolls tend to mar the otherwise symmetrical proportions of this maker's instruments. Label as
follows :

AlessandriGagliano Alomnus
Stradivarius fecit Neapoli anno 1701

GAGLIANO, GENNARO, son of Allessandro, born about 1695, died 1750. He is considered
the best maker of the family, and his instruments
are, as a consequence, much sought after. He exercised great care in the selection of his wood, and
used a much finer varnish than either his father or
brother Nicolas. Whether or not he was a prolific

maker is uncertain, but instruments of his are rarely to be met with.

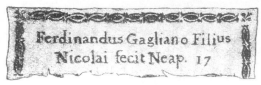

GAGLIANO, NICOLAS, another son of Allessandro, was born about 1665, died 1740. He was a finer workman than his father, paying more attention to the outward appearance of the instrument, the tone of which is pronounced very fine in his best examples. Besides violins he made a large number of violas and violoncellos. His tickets usually run : "Nicolaus Gagliano filius Alexandri fecit Neap."

The remaining members of the family are : Ferdinando, born 1706, died 1781, eldest son of Nicolas; Guiseppe, died 1793; Giovanni, died 1806, also sons of Nicolas; Raffael and Antonio, sons of Giovanni. Antonio died in 1860. Label of Ferdinando :

GRANCINO, PAOLO, 1665-90, was instructed by and worked under Nicolas Amati. His instruments are of large model, light yellow varnish, large sound-holes, negligent purfling, and carelessly finished corners. The arching is flattish, and the scrolls coarse. The tone of his instruments, however, possess great power and is of good quality. Other members of the family worked in Milan.

GRANCINO, GIOVANNI BATTISTA, a good maker of the same school, probably a son of Paolo. Label as follows:

Gia.Bapt.Grancino in Contrada Largha di Milano anno 1695

GUADAGNINI, LORENZO, Placentia, 1695-1760. This maker worked for several years with Stradivarius, whose instruments he copied with more or less success. The wood chosen was generally of fine quality, and the workmanship is evidence that the maker fabricated his instruments with extreme care. The tone of a genuine Lorenzo is most brilliant in the upper register, but somewhat weak in the lower. They are much sought after by performers where the possession of a Cremona of the first order is unattainable. The varnish used was a rich amber or yellowish red of fine quality. A ticket of this maker is as follows :

Lavrentius Guadagnini Pater,
& alumnus Antonj Straduarj
fecit Placentie Anno 174?

GUADAGNINI, GIOVANNI BATTISTA,

was a brother of Lorenzo. He made some really good instruments, dividing his attention between the Stradivari and the Amati models. Giambattista was a son of Lorenzo, and reputed pupil of Stradivarius. He afterwards went to Piacenza and subsequently settled in Turin. His instruments are also much prized. Guiseppe, son of Giovanni, worked successively in Milan, Como and Parma. Other members of the same family also made violins, but little appears to be known of them or of their works.

> Joannes Baptifta Guadagnini Pla-
> centinus fecit Mediolani 17 0 3

> Joannes Baptifta Guadagnini ☩
> Cremonenfis fecit Taurini.   GBG
> nnus Antoni Stradivari 17

GUARNERIUS, ANDREAS, born about 1626, died 1698.

The founder of this celebrated family of violin makers was a pupil of Nicolas Amati. His instruments are estimable for good workmanship somewhat in the style of the Amati, although marked by certain peculiar details, by which indeed they are recognised. His varnish is either golden yellow or brownish red. Andreas left two sons, Peter and Joseph.

Ticket as follows:

> Andreas Guarnerius fecit Cremonæ fub
> titulo Sanctæ Terefiæ 16

GUARNERIUS, GIUSEPPE, usually called
"Joseph," son of Andreas, born 1666, died about
1739. Although he may have been a pupil of Andreas, he has not followed his model. Some say he
followed Stradivarius, whose contemporary he was,
and subsequently followed his cousin, also called
Joseph, of whom we shall speak presently. He has
consequently varied both in his patterns and in the
details of manufacture; but his instruments are of
good quality and much esteemed, and are more ele-
gant in form than those of his father. The colour
of his varnish is a brilliant red.

A ticket of his reads :

Ioſeph Guarnerius filius Andreæ fecit
Cremone ſub titulo S. Tereſie 17 06

GUARNERIUS, JOSEPH ANTHONY,
the most renowned of this family, was born in 1683
and died about 1745; his period of activity dating
from 1725. According to M. Fétis, his father was
John Baptist Guarnerius, who was a brother of
Andreas.

He is usually known by the surname of "del Jesù," because many of his labels bear this device.

✠

I.H.S.

Most authorities agree in dividing his working career into four periods. His first attempts were not marked by any characteristic sign of originality, except in the indifferent choice of material, form and in the varnish. In the second period, his instruments are found to be made with care; the wood used for the sides and back being of excellent quality, and cut on the quarter *(sur maille);* the deal of the belly has been well chosen; the varnish of fine complexion and elastic quality. The pattern is small, but of beautiful outline. The arching is slightly elevated and falls off towards the purfling in a graceful curve. M. Fétis in his criticism of these instruments, points out an obvious defect, namely, the too great thickness of the wood, especially in the backs, which tends to impede the freedom of vibration, and consequently the brilliance of sound. In the third or grand period of his career, Joseph Guarnerius, says the same authority, presents a still more surprising variety in the forms of his instruments. During this period he produced instruments of large pattern, made of excellent wood cut *(sur maille);* and conformably to the best conditions possible, in respect to arching and degrees of thickness. A beautiful varnish of a lovely orange shade, remarkable for its fineness and elasticity, protect these excellent instruments, which are considered equal to the most beautiful productions of Anthony Stradivarius. We now arrive at the fourth period, which, it is sad to observe, forms a striking contrast to the glorious third. Here we have evidence of a lamentable falling off. The master seems to have worked carelessly, the wood is poor, as is the varnish.

Reports have been handed down to account for this apparent degeneration of talent, but as it is impossible to verify the same, it can serve no good purpose to here relate them. It only remains to be said, concerning this great master, that he has built up a reputation that is not likely to suffer by mere rumour.

Paganini possessed one of the finest examples of a del Jesù, which was presented to him by a M. Liv-

ron, a French merchant of Leghorn. At his death,
27th May, 1840, Paganini bequeathed it to his native
town, Genoa, where it is preserved in a glass case in
the museum.

> Joſeph Guarnerius fecit ✠
> Cremonæ anno 17   IHS

GUARNERIUS, PIETRO, Cremona, eldest
son of Andreas, born 1655, and lived to an advanced
age. His first productions, which are of flat model,
are dated from Cremona, but later on he established
himself at Mantua, where he manufactured a great
quantity of instruments of undoubted merit, but
have the fault of too high an arching, and some
there are wanting in brilliancy of tone. His tickets
usually run:

> Petrus Guarnerius Cremonenſis fecit
> Mantuæ fub.tit.Sanctæ Terefiæ 1695

This maker had a nephew also called Pietro, who
worked at Mantua from about 1725 to 1740, and

subsequently in Venice till about 1755. He was a pupil of his uncle, but his work is less esteemed.

LANDOLPHUS, CARLO, Milan, 1750-1775, reputed pupil of Guarnerius. This maker was decidedly original in his pattern. Although his instruments are not characteristic of great beauty as regards outline, they possess a very pleasing tone. He is one of the last of the old Italian school, con- sequently his instruments are rapidly increasing in value. The most striking point observable in his work is the extremely weak and small scroll. He left a number of instruments unpurfled and otherwise in an unfinished state. Those with the light red varnish are considered the best. He also made some violoncellos of small size. Ticket :

Carolus Ferdinandus Landulphus
Fecit Mediolani in Via St. Margaritae
Anno '755.

MAGGINI, GIOVANNI PAOLO, born 1580, died about 1640. This distinguished maker is the second representative of the Brescian school, and reputed pupil of Gasparo da Salo. According to recent researches, Maggini was born in Botticino Sera, a small village not far from Brescia.

Maggini's instruments are in general of large pattern; their proportions are similar to those of Gasparo da Salo, and the style of workmanship almost identical. The swell or arching is decided, and reaches almost to the edges. The sides or ribs are narrow; the bellies very strong and of good quality, the backs generally thin, with the wood cut on the layers. The varnish, which is remarkable for its delicacy, is of a yellowish light brown colour; sometimes, however, he used a brownish red varnish. In either case it is of excellent quality. The extended dimensions, and the proportion of the arching relative to the various thicknesses of the wood, impart to most of these instruments a superb, grave and melancholy tone.

Another characteristic of this master's productions is found in his ornamentation. He generally affected a double row of purfling and various other decorations, and although Maggini was not alone in this respect, he appears to be the last maker who relinquished the practice of introducing any ornate addition, which, anterior to his period, was considered so essential to the finish of an instrument.

Maggini is credited with being the first maker who paid any real attention to the inside of the instrument, having, it is said, introduced the side linings and corner blocks, which have ever since been a *sine qua non* of construction.

De Beriot, the great violinist, was an admirer of Maggini's violins.

Tickets of this celebrated maker are not dated. The following is a copy of one :

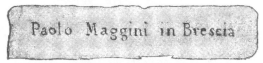

MONTAGNANA, DOMINIC, Cremona and Venice, 1700-1740. He was probably a pupil of Nicolas Amati, whose model he at first copied, but subsequently modified this for one of his own, of a somewhat large pattern. The scroll is larger and more powerful than that of his reputed master and in the sound holes he also differs. As regards the arching and outline, the Amati type is at once apparent. The varnish is superb, and of golden brown transparency. The wood chosen is always the very finest, and the workmanship is all that can be desired. He also made some very fine violoncellos His best instruments, which are of great rarity, are dated from Venice.

RUGERI, FRANCESCO (Ruger or Ruggeri), Cremona, 1670-1720. This excellent maker was a pupil and follower of Nicolas Amati (some writers say Hieronymus). His instruments are much sought after, and, as a consequence, are extensively copied and passed off as genuine. His varnish is generally dark golden brown.

RUGERI, GIAM-BATTISTA, supposed to be a brother of the foregoing, pupil of Amati, born at Cremona, 1660. He subsequently went to Brescia.

where he worked from about 1670 to the end of the
century.   Ticket :

Io: Bap. Rogerius Bon: Nicolai Amati de Cremona alumnus Brixiæ fecit Anno Domini 1671

SALO, GASPARO DA (or Gasparo di Berto-
lotti), born 1542, died 1612. This is the earliest
maker of whom any reliable record is extant.   He is
said to have been born at Salo in Lombardy, and
afterwards to have settled in Brescia.   Gasparo is
generally credited with the honour of inventing or
producing violins in their present shape. · He seems
to have devoted his early period to the manufacture
of lutes and viols, and subsequently to have turned
his attention to the violin, which he greatly improved,
thereby founding the Brescian school of violin
makers; the earliest known.   The violins of Gasparo
which have now become very scarce, do not, it is true,
exhibit that indication of finish so observable in the
instruments produced by his reputed pupil, Maggini,
but his model is excellent and the tone good, being
somewhat analogous to that of the tenor.   The fact

that Gasparo never dated his labels, makes it difficult to determine with certainty the exact period of
his activity.

Facsimile label as follows :

Gasparo da Salò, In Brescia.

SERAPHIN, SANCTUS (Santo Seraphino),
1710-1748, worked in Venice, and is considered one
of the most careful and painstaking makers of the
Italian school. His wood is beautifully figured and
well selected. His purfling is excellent, and he used
a fine brilliant varnish. He usually branded his instruments near the button. Ticket as follows :

Sanctus Seraphin
Utinenfis Fecit
Venetijs Ann. 17

STORIONI, LORENZO, Cremona, 1780-
1798. The last of the old Cremonese school.   He
sometimes copied Joseph "del Jesù," at others, he
followed his own originality.   His instruments exhibit great variation; notably in the position of the
sound holes, which he never placed twice alike.   He
used a poor varnish which clearly indicates the
change of process which was then taking place.
Although these instruments are far from being
graceful in outline or beautiful in appearance, they
are capable of producing a good tone; in fact, in
Italy a good Storioni is highly spoken of.   This
maker does not appear to have made many violas or
violoncellos.   Ticket :

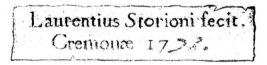

Laurentius Storioni fecit.
Cremonæ 17...

STRADIVARIUS, ANTONIO, the king of
fiddle makers, born at Cremona, 1644, died 1737.
This great master was an apprentice in the workshop
of Nicolas Amati.   At the age of twenty-three years
he produced some violins, the exact reproductions of

his master, and into which it is said he placed the
labels of Nicolas. In the year 1670 he signed his
instruments with his own name. From that date,
until about 1690, he produced but few instruments,
and it is conjectured, that during this period of
twenty years, his labours and researches were more
in the nature of experiments than of commercial
enterprise.

From the year 1690 the individuality of Stradivarius began to assert itself. It was then that he
began to give greater amplitude to his model. He
reduced the high arching hitherto prevailing, and
determined with much nicety the various thicknesses
of wood, but he still retained many of the chief
characteristics of his master The productions of
this period are called " Long Strads." From 1700
to 1725 Stradivarius was in the full lustre of his
fame. During this period he made those master-
pieces known as the " Grand Pattern." " He no
longer felt his way, but being certain of all that he
did, he carried his manufacture, even to the minutest
details, to the highest possible finish, especially with

regard to the varnish, the quality of which is fine and extremely supple."

"The workmanship of the interior of the instru ment displays no less perfection; all is there finished with the greatest care. The degrees of thickness are adjusted in a rational manner, and are remarkable for a precision which could not have been attained except by long study and experiment. The back, the belly, and all the parts of which the instrument is composed, are in a perfectly harmonious relation. It was, doubtless, repeated trials and diligent observations, which also led Stradivarius, throughout this period of his productive career, to make the blocks and sides of his violins of willow, the specific lightness of which surpasses that of every other wood. In short, everything had been foreseen, calculated, and determined with certainty, in these admirable instruments. The bar alone is too weak, in consequence of the gradual rise in the pitch, from the beginning of the eighteenth century; the inevitable result of which has been a considerable increase of tension, and a much greater pressure exercised on the belly. Hence the necessity has arisen for re-

barring all the old violins and violoncellos." Such
is Fétis's description of this grand period.

From 1725 to 1730, Stradivarius produced fewer
instruments than he had previously done in the same
period of time. Although they are very good, the
workmanship no longer displays the same perfection. The arching becomes more rounded, which
tends to impair the clearness of the sound, and the
varnish is brown.

After the year 1730, the master exhibits a decided
falling off. Stradivarius, in his eighty-sixth year,
still, however, continued at his bench, assisted by his
two sons, Omobono and Francisco, and his pupil,
Carlo Bergonzi, who partially, if not wholly, kept
the business going. Stradivarius signed many of his
instruments as having been made simply under his
direction. After the death of this great maker, many
instruments which remained unfinished in his workshop were completed by his sons. Most of these instruments bear the father's name.

Stradivarius died at the great age of ninety-three
years, and he was buried in the Cathedral of
Cremona.

Facsimile of a written ticket :

Facsimile of a printed ticket :

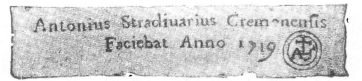

STRADIVARIUS, FRANCISCO, Cremona,
born 1671, died 1743. **STRADIVARIUS, OMOBONO,** born 1679, died 1742. These two were sons and pupils of the great Stradivarius, and the only members who followed their father's calling, with whom they worked until his death; the father during the latter period of his life, signing the instruments "sub disciplinâ Antonii Stradivarius." After the death of their illustrious father, they each worked on their own account. Francisco is reputed to have manufacturegd some good violins from 1725 to 1740; his brother chiefly occupying

himself in repairing. The productions, however, of
these two brothers sink into insignificance when com-
pared with those of their renowned father.

> Francifcus Stradivarius Cremonenſis
> Filius Antonii faciebat Anno 17 4 ?

> Omobonus Stradiuarius figlij Antony
> Cremone Fecit Anno 1740 ⫏

TECHLER, DAVID, Rome, 1680-1740. He is
said by some to be a pupil of Stainer, from the fact
that he produced instruments of that type. He
first worked at Salzburg, then at Venice, and finally
at Rome, where he gained much experience. Instruments of this latter city are of the Italian model.
His work proves him to have been a careful and
studious maker. The varnish is usually deep yellow. Label:

> David Tecchler Liutaro
> Fecit Romæ Anno 1703.

TESTORE, CARLO GUISEPPE, Cremona.

Flourished 1690-1720. He produced instruments of good quality both as regards finish and tone; his model being Guarnerius. His instruments are eagerly sought after by those who desire to become possessed of a good old Italian instrument, but are unwilling or unable to give a fancy price. These instruments are, however, gradually rising in value.

TESTORE, CARLO ANTONIO, Milan, 1730, and TESTORE, PAOLO ANTONIO, Milan, 1740, sons of Carlo Guiseppe.

They made excellent instruments after the model of their father, and the tone is good. Paolo frequently left his instruments unpurfled.

Carlo Antonio Teftore figlio maggiore
del fu Carlo Giufeppe in Contrada lar-
ga al fegno dell' Aquila Milano 1741

II.—GERMAN AND TYROLESE.

BACHMANN, CARL LUDWIG, of Berlin (1716-1800). This maker was one of the most celebrated of the German school. He made his instruments rather strong in the wood, but now that age has been at work on them, they possess the advantage of being formed into first-class instruments by skilful repairers.

BENTE, MATTEO. A maker of the Brescian school, flourished about 1580. He made some good violins, which are chiefly to be found in collections.

BUCHSTETTER, GABRIEL DAVID, a native of Ratisbon, flourished in the latter part of the eighteenth century. He copied the Cremonese makers and used a brown varnish. His wood is rather coarse-grained, consequently his instruments are not very highly esteemed.

BUCHSTETTER, JOSEPHUS, son of Gabriel David. Made some instruments of good quality and tone, and adopted a flat model.

EBERLE, ULRIC, of Prague, about 1750, an eminent German maker, whose instruments at one time were considered nearly equal to the best Italian makers.

HELMER, CHARLES (CAROLUS), of Prague, a pupil of Eberle. He made some very fine instruments. Otto says: "They have, however, the fault that the three upper strings improve greatly by being played on, but the G string, in most of them, remains so far inferior, that while the tone of the former is such as may be expected from a full sized violin, that of the latter only resembles a child's toy-instrument. Yet an experienced maker would find no difficulty in correcting this fault."

HOFFMANN, MARTIN, one of the earliest representatives of the German school, flourished in Leipzig in the latter part of the seventeenth century. He was better known as a lute-maker. He made violins possessing excellent tone, but they do not find much favour by reason of their ungainly appearance.

JAUCH (or **JAUG**)**,** of Dresden, early part of eighteenth century. The best description of this maker's instruments is that contained in Otto's treatise. ":Jauch," he says, "has manufactured very good violins on the model of the Cremonese, and displayed, in his beautiful and excellent workman-ship, a thorough knowledge of the wood, and of the due proportions of strength required in the respective parts of the instrument. But his violins produce a very weak squally tone, when they have been carelessly repaired; though even in this case they may be often restored and brought nearly to equal the Italian, by placing them in the hands of an experienced maker, possessing a knowledge of mathematics and acoustics, without which they will be completely spoiled."

KLOTZ FAMILY. This group represent well-nigh a century of activity, i.e., from about 1670 to about 1760.

KLOTZ, EGIDIUS. Born in Mittenwald. When young he quitted his native village and placed himself under Stainer at Absam. Having learnt the art under this celebrated maker, he returned to his native place and set up in business on his own account, and soon gained considerable renown as a maker of superior instruments, so much so that his productions for some time almost eclipsed those of his master. Even now a sound specimen—which is rarely seen, is not lightly passed over. His instruments possess a fine and powerful tone.

KLOTZ, MATHIAS, 1653-1745. Worked for about twenty years in Mittenwald, during which period he produced instruments of an unsatisfactory nature. He appears to have been aware of this, and with the object of increasing his knowledge, he undertook a journey to Florence and Cremona and other centres of violin industry. With his newly-acquired experience he returned to his native place and established himself in rather a large way.

KLOTZ, SEBASTIAN, son of Mathias (1700-1760). The instruments of this maker are a decided improvement, both as regards pattern and tone. He adopted a somewhat flat model and coated his instruments with a superior varnish to

that previously used by the family. His instruments are highly valued.

Sebaſtian Kloz, in Mittenwald.

With regard to the other members of the family,
great confusion exists in the minds of writers as to
how they stood in point of relationship one with the
other. In name they are: George (1723-1797), Joseph
(1730-1760), Joan Carol (about 1780), Michael (about
the same period).

Spurious instruments bearing the name of Klotz
or Clotz flood the market, and the uninitiated should
regard them with grave suspicion, unless or until the
advice of a competent expert has been obtained as
to their genuineness or otherwise.

RAUCH, THOMAS, of Breslau. Made some
very good violins in the early part of the eighteenth
century. He worked on an original model, and made
instruments noted for their powerful tone.

RUPPERT, of Erfurt, a maker who worked on
an extremely original model. He made all his in-

struments very flat in model, and dispensed with the side linings and corner blocks, and omitted the purfling. The front and back tables were, however, made with due regard to thicknesses, which redeemed them somewhat from the defects above mentioned. The instruments possess a good tone and fine examples are highly priced.

SCHEINLEIN, MATTHIAS FREDERICK, of Langenfeld (1730-1771). Made fine instruments which, in his time, were in great demand. He made them too weak, consequently many of them are now practically spoiled by subsequent repairing.

STAINER, JACOBUS, born at Hall, near Absam—a short distance from Innsbruck—July 14, 1621, died at Absam, 1683. This maker is the most renowned of the German school, concerning whose early career the following account has been handed down. A priest residing in the district of Absam took a fancy to young Jacob, and had him sent to Innsbruck to learn the art of organ building under one Daniel Herz. This calling not suiting the youth's inclinations, his master advised him to learn the art of violin making. Stainer then went to Cremona, and

placed himself under Nicolas Amati, who soon re-
recognised the talent of his young pupil, and took
great pains in instructing him in the secrets of the
art. He then quitted Cremona, and for a short time
worked in Venice under Vermercati, who at that time
was a maker of some merit. With an accumu-
lation of experience gained in the best schools of
the time, Stainer finally returned to Absam and
settled there as a maker of violins on his own account. In the year 1645 he married a Margaretha
Holzhammer, by whom he had several children. His
renown as a violin maker rapidly increased, but for
some reason or other he found it difficult to provide
for the wants of himself and family, and he was
compelled to travel about the country in order to
dispose of his instruments. However, in 1658, he
was appointed court violin maker to the Archduke
Leopold, and in 1669 received the distinction of
"Maker to the Emperor"; but all these advantages
and honours contributed but little to raise him from
his chronic state of poverty. He now began to experience some bitter reverses. A certain creditor of
his, named Solomon Heubnar, with whom he at one

time lived (Stainer left him without paying for his board) lodged an information against him charging him with the crime of heresy. He was seized and thrown into prison, and remained there six months, at the expiration of which he found himself utterly ruined and poverty stared him in the face. He was then persecuted by Count Albert Fugger for certain dues which it was customary to levy on court trades-men. Stainer petitioned the Emperor to waive this claim, but to no purpose, his supplication being ig-nored, it is thought, in consequence of his previous conviction for the alleged heresy. Stainer then fell into a state of abject misery, neglected his work, and finally died out of mind. It will therefore be seen that this renowned maker worked under most distressing conditions, and it is a marvel that he was able to produce anything worthy of subsequent copying. Stainer's house is still pointed out, and, it is said, the bench to which he was bound when mad.

Another story which has gained currency in some quarters, but in others said to be mythical, recounts that at the latter period of his life he abandoned his calling and became an inmate of a Benedictine monastery. Here, with the assistance of a brother monk, he contrived to get together sufficient materials for the manufacture of sixteen violins of great beauty. These apparently fabulous fiddles are known as the "Elector" Stainers from the circumstance that each Elector was supposed to be the recipient of one of these instruments, the remaining going to the Emperor of Germany. For information concerning the instruments made by this unfortunate fiddle maker, the best is that contained in the treatise of Jacob Augustus Otto, maker to the Court of the Archduke of Weimar, translated from the German by Thomas Fardely, of Leeds (1833), and since then by the late Mr. Bishop, of Cheltenham (William Reeves, London).

Otto says: "The instruments made by Jacob Stainer differ from the Cremonese both in outward shape and in tone. They are higher modelled, and their proportions of strength are calculated quite differently. The nearest comparison which can be drawn between a Cremonese and a Stainer is this: a Cremonese has a strong reedy, sonorous tone something similar to that of a clarionet, while a Stainer approaches to that of a flute. The belly is modelled higher than the back. The highest part of the model under the bridge extends exactly one half of the instrument towards the lower broad part and then diminishes towards the end edge. It decreases in a like manner at the upper broad part towards the neck. The breadth of this model is uniformly the same as that of the bridge, from which it diminishes towards the side edge. The edges are very strong and round. The purfling lies somewhat nearer to the edges than in the Cremonese, and is likewise narrower than in the latter (the Cremonese) in which it is very broad. The *f* holes in Stainer instruments are very beautifully cut, and the upper and under turns are perfectly circular. In length they are somewhat shorter than the Cremonese. The neck is particularly handsome, and the scroll is as round and smooth as if it had been turned. Some few have lions' heads, which are extremely well carved. The sides and the back are made of the finest figured maple and covered with a deep yellow amber varnish. In some the screw (peg) box is varnished dark brown and the belly deep yellow. The above are the most accurate marks by which the genuine Stainer instruments may be distinguished. They are rarely to be found with any labels inside, but in the few which are to be met with of the genuine instruments bearing any inscription, they are simply written, not printed. In the Tyrolese imitations of Stainers they are all printed. In the genuine Cremonese instruments they are likewise invariably printed."

Genuine Stainers with labels have this written inscription : " Jacobus Stainer in Absam prope Œnipontum h-fis 165-." The following is a facsimile :

III.—FRENCH.

BOQUAY, JACQUES. Paris, about 1700-
1735. One of the earliest of the old French school.
Under whom he learnt the art of violin making is
not known, but his instruments, as also those of his
contemporaries, clearly indicate that the Italian influence was suffusing itself in no uncertain manner.
It appears that about the middle of the sixteenth
century, one Nicolas Rénault, a French viol and
lute maker, travelled into Italy and became associ-
ated with Andreas Amati, and even assisted that
maker in the manufacture of certain instruments for
the chapel of Charles IX, in 1566, and, after a somewhat lengthened stay in Italy, he returned to France
the gainer of considerable experience. Here, per-
haps, may be the explanation why Boquay and the
rest of the early French school principally adhered

to the Amati model. Later on Boquay sought to become original, notably with regard to the sound holes and the scroll. The tone is sweet, but lacks power.

JACQUES BOQUAY
RUE DARGENTTUIL
A PARIS, 17

COMBLE, AMBROISE DE, Tourney, Belgium (1730-1760). The best maker of the old French school, and reputed pupil of Stradivarius. Although the instruments of de Comble cannot be said to be on the model adopted by the great Cremonese maker during his best period, there is nevertheless some indication to lead to the belief that he endeavoured to follow the renowned artist in the matter of varnish. In this respect he was fairly successful. His instruments are rather flat and of large pattern, somewhat on the lines of Stradivarius's later productions, and although they are not characteristic of refined workmanship, the material chosen was of the best quality. He made his instruments strong in the wood, consequently they possess a very full and rich tone. De Comble also made some excellent violoncellos.

LUPOT, NICOLAS, born at Stuttgart, 1758, died in Paris, 1824, founder of the modern school of violin making. His father, also a maker of some merit, removed to Orléans in the year 1770, and in this town instructed his son in the art which was destined to make his name famous. During his pupilage Nicolas set himself to study the instruments of the great Italian makers, especially those of Stradivarius, and in the result he elected to adopt the model of this master, from which he seldom, if ever, departed. With such diligence and enthusiasm did he labour to produce something akin to his ideal that he soon was able to turn out an instrument that suffered but little on comparison with the Italians of the first water. Thus a most beneficial influence in the art of violin making became propagated. In 1798 Nicolas quitted Orléans for Paris and established himself in business, and there for twenty-six years he carried on a labour of love which, as well, produced considerable pecuniary benefits. Lupot had not been long in Paris before his work claimed the attention of the Conservatoire, then but recently formed, and he was accordingly

appointed violin maker to that excellent institution :
he was similarly appointed to the Chapel Royal. It
is not difficult to imagine that Lupot endeavoured
to revive the lost art of making the old Italian
varnish, judging from the various qualities with
which he was wont to cover his instruments. In this
respect, however, he cannot be said to have been successful, but what he did use ranks high as a modern
varnish. The instruments of this maker are highly
prized, especially those made between 1805 and 1824.
An impetus was probably given to the value of
Lupot's violins from the circumstance that the celebrated Spohr played for a long time on a Lupot,
the tone of which he declared was " full and powerful"; in fact, the great virtuoso only parted with
this instrument on becoming possessed of a Strad.
Lupot appears to have been almost as uncertain
about his labels as he was concerning his varnish.
At Orléans he adopted a Latinised inscription, and
in Paris, three labels have been noticed variously
worded. The following are copies of some
labels :

N. Lupot fils, Luthier, rue d'Illiers, à Orléans, l'an 17—.

Nicholas Lupot, Luthier, rue de Grammont, à Paris, l'an 17—.

Nicholas Lupot, rue Croix des petits champs, à Paris, l'an 1817.

Nicholas had a brother named François, who be came celebrated as a maker of bows.

VUILLAUME, JOHN BAPTISTE, born at Mirecourt, October 7, 1798, died February 19, 1875; the greatest violin maker and copier of modern times. It is not precisely known under whom he received his first instruction in the art of violin making. Some say his father, one Claude Vuillaume, born at Mirecourt in 1771, died 1834, whilst others maintain that the father was not a fiddle maker, but a carrier between Mirecourt and Nancy. At all events, at the age of nineteen, he was engaged by François Chanot, a violin maker of repute, who had just about that period established a workshop for the manufacture of a new-shaped violin, which had been patented, so it is not unlikely that François Chanot was his first real master. He next en-

gaged himself with one Lété, an organ builder, who
dealt in violins, and ultimately became a partner in
the concern. In 1828 he parted from Lété and continued in business alone. During this period he
found great difficulty in disposing of his instruments; the rage being for those of Italian manufacture. He thereupon took to fabricating copies of
the old masters, and his operations in this line appear to have been attended with great success. As
a large number of old instruments, Italian and
others, passed through his hands for repair, Vuillaume had ample opportunity afforded him for
studying and ascertaining the inward and outward
conditions necessary for the production of good
tone, and this advantage he was not slow to avail
himself of. Fortified with a vast amount of experience, combined with much knowledge gained by experiment, Vuillaume was in course of time enabled
to produce an instrument in all but one point equal
to the greatest Italian masters, the condition wanting being that of age. In some cases, possibly
through stress of trade, Vuillaume endeavoured to
supply this deficiency by giving to his instruments

an appearance of wear and long usage. In his latter years, however, he relinquished this pernicious practice. The climax of his skill as a copyist was reached on the occasion when he reproduced a facsimile of Paganini's famous Guarnerius, entrusted for repair. This copy was so marvellous in its similarity with the original, both as regards appearance and tone, that the great virtuoso himself failed to recognise his own instrument, and Vuillaume had to point it out to him. In addition to his high capabilities as a violin maker, Vuillaume was renowned as a bow maker, and effected some improvements in that important adjunct, and on the whole proved himself a genius of uncommon order.

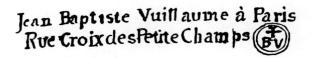

IV.—BRITISH.

WILLIAM ADDISON—THOMAS COLE — EDWARD PAMPHILON — PEMBERTON—THOMAS URQUHART—CHRISTOPHER WISE.

THIS group represents the early English school and the principal makers existing during the seventeenth century. It may reasonably be inferred that they were more at home with the viol than with the violin as known to-day. Little can be said concerning their early productions, as they are now all but extinct; a great portion of them probably perished in the great fire of London in 1666, in which city some of them were supposed to have worked.

Christopher Wise is said to have made some fairly good instruments of a highly decorative nature.

Jacob Rayman was the better artist, and some instruments attributed to him reflect great credit on this early school.

Thomas Urquhart was a still further advance, his outline and varnish places him in the front rank of the period.

Edward Pamphilon made instruments of a very tubby appearance, but they are said to possess a clear and penetrating tone; age, too, has imparted a very rich colouring to the varnish.

Several other names have been handed down, but as they are minus the instruments, nothing of importance can be said on the subject.

Aldred and Bolles are mentioned in Mace's "Musick's Monument."

ADDISON, WILLIAM, was a maker of viols and early violins in the middle of the seventeenth century. He worked in Moorfields, London.

AIRETON, EDMUND. A London maker about the middle of the eighteenth century. He copied successively the instruments of Stainer, Amati and Stradivarius, but those on the Amati model are most admired.

BANKS FAMILY. They rank among the best makers of English violins, and genuine specimens are eagerly sought after and realise good prices.

BANKS, BENJAMIN. Born July 14, 1727, died February 18, 1795. Accounts differ as to the place of his birth, but as his parents were living in Salisbury in the year 1725, it is generally supposed he was born in that town.

Banks has been justly termed "the English Amati," and this comparison is well deserved. His fiddles are faithful copies of the great Italian, both as to model and varnish. These instruments are, however, very rare, and fiddles of this model offered as genuine Benjamins should only be purchased with the advice of experts.

Benjamin also made instruments for the then well-known music-firm of Longman and Broderip in London. These were made on a different model, somewhat after the Stainer model, and they are greatly inferior to his favourite Amati fiddles, the finish and varnish indicate hurry and carelessness. These fiddles are labelled with the name of the firm

for whom he worked. I have seen many fiddles
bearing the name of Longman and Broderip and
said to have been made by Benjamin Banks. The
majority of them are, however, spurious. It has
been the custom of many dealers to cut off the name
of Longman and Broderip from the bottom of the
published music of that firm and insert these in
fiddles, and as Benjamin Banks was known to have
worked for them, some show of genuineness is
thereby implied.

Banks made a number of violas and violoncellos.
The latter instruments stand pre-eminent for workmanship and tone and are particularly well adapted
for the performance of solo and chamber music.
This maker adopted a variety of methods for stamp-
ing and otherwise labelling his instruments. Below
the button was the favourite place.

The labels mostly seen are :

Made by Benjamin Banks, Catherine Street,
Salisbury.

Benjamin Banks, fecit Salisbury.

Benjamin Banks, Musical Instrument Maker, In
Catherine Street, Salisbury.

B. Banks, Sarum. "B. B." stamped under the button.

The varnish used by Banks varied from a deep red to a yellow brown.

One word of advice, beware of the unredeemed pledge.

BANKS, BENJAMIN. Son of the preceding; born at Salisbury, 1754, died in Liverpool, 1820. He worked at first for his renowned father, afterwards removing to London, where, possibly, he assisted in making the Longman and Broderip instruments. He then went to Liverpool and worked there until his death. Very little is known of him or his works, though it is possible that many of his instruments have been passed off as the work of his father.

BANKS, JAMES and **HENRY,** two other sons of the great Benjamin, and successors to the business at Salisbury, where they were both born, James about 1756, died 1831; Henry, 1770, died 1830.

James was the violin maker of the concern, while Henry devoted himself to tuning pianofortes and

repairing instruments. Sometimes, however, they
collaborated in the production of violins and violoncellos. They also extended the sphere of their operations to music selling and dealt in other musical
instruments. The fame of the Banks family as
violin makers declined at this period.

BARRETT, JOHN. A London maker, who
worked about 1725. He made some good instruments which are dated from the Harp and Crown in
Piccadilly. He followed the Stainer model. His
varnish is unsatisfactory.

BETTS, JOHN, London, born at Stamford in
1755, died 1823. This excellent maker was a pupil
of Duke, and adopted the Amati model. He was
not himself a prolific maker, his time being principally occupied in the study of old Italian instruments, the result of which enabled him to become a
very successful dealer and connoisseur. Betts, or
"old John," as he was most commonly called, carried on an extensive business in the construction of
violins, and employed in his workshop such men as
John Carter, Edward Betts, Panormo, Bernhard
Fendt, all of whom subsequently succeeded in

making good instruments on their own account.
Betts's shop was No. 2 near Northgate of the Royal
Exchange, and after his death the business was continued by his descendants till within a few years
ago.

DUKE, RICHARD, London, about 1765-1791.
Probably no violin of English make has attained
such popularity as have the instruments of this
maker, hence it is that he is so extensively imitated.
Who instructed him in the art of making violins,
etc., is not positively known, but his instruments are
of the highest order in all respects but the varnish,
in which he was not always successful. Duke followed both the Stainer and Amati models, the latter
being his best. His violoncellos are rather high in
model, long in pattern, yellowish varnish and rich
in tone. For his violins he used a dull brown varnish, very elastic and transparent. During a considerable period Duke worked in the vicinity of
Holborn. Many of his instruments are stamped near
the button "Duke, London."

Labels, mostly written in pen and ink, are as
follows :

Richd. Duke, Londini, fecit 1767.

Richard Duke, Maker, Holborn, London, Anno 1777.

The following is a copy of a printed one :

"Richard Duke, Maker, near opposite Great Turn-Stile, Holbourn, London."

FENDT, BERNHARD, born at Inspruck, in the Tyrol, in 1756, died in London in 1832. He was at first instructed in the art of violin making by his uncle in Paris, who spelt his name Fent, a maker there of some reputation. Bernhard then came to London and entered the service of Thomas Dodd, the bow maker, and remained with him several years, working in conjunction with John Frederick Lott. They were never entrusted to carry their work beyond the white, and the instruments turned out by this pair were delivered to their master, who applied the varnish with his own hand, the secret of which he kept carefully to himself.

FORSTER, WILLIAM, known as "Old" Forster, born at Brampton, Cumberland, May, 1739, died in London, December 14, 1808. The name of Forster in connection with violin making

8

includes a family whose operation extended over a very considerable period, but the artist under notice was *the* fiddle maker of the group, and his instruments to-day reflect great credit on the British school of a century ago; indeed his instruments, whether they be violins, violas or violoncellos, are pre-eminent amongst the productions of this country. His father pursued two occupations, viz., that of spinning-wheel maker and violin maker and repairer; instructions in which handicrafts were duly imparted to the son, who also became tolerably proficient as a violinist. In consequence of some family differences, the young man quitted his native village and proceeded to London, arriving there in 1759. His first endeavours in the metropolis were unsuccessful, and he was forced to accept some employment offered him by a gun-stock maker. However, he did not forsake the art he loved, and his spare time was occupied in making violins, which he disposed of to the music shops. During this time he suffered great hardship and privation, the effects of which were never afterwards entirely eradicated. At length he obtained employ-

ment as a violin maker at a music shop on Tower
Hill kept by one Beck, and the violins he made
during his two years' engagement there, gaining
much recognition, he not unnaturally demanded an
advance in wages. This was refused, and Forster
consequently left him. In 1762 he commenced business on his own account at a house in Duke's Court,
and there his artistic abilities procured for him the
attention and patronage of the musical dilettanti.
He then moved into St. Martin's Lane, and added
music publishing and selling to his business, and at
this period he was wont to cut his name from the
title-pages of his soiled or unsold music and use it
as a ticket for his instruments. In 1781 he entered
into negotiations with Haydn for the supply and
publication of certain pieces of music for the string
family, which resulted, it would appear, in a great
success all round. About 1784, Forster opened in
the Strand—No. 348, and here the climax of his success was attained, even to the extent of receiving
Royal patronage. From the year 1762 to 1770 he
adopted the Stainer model, and applied to his instruments some sort of dark stain, completing the

operation with a coat of varnish. From 1770 or thereabouts he affected the Amati pattern with greater success, and this refers particularly to his violoncellos, as they are really grand instruments, better varnish is used and greater attention is paid to detail. Robert Lindley, the famous violoncellist, used one of Forster's instruments at the Italian Opera for nearly forty years; he named it " The Eclipse." Crossdill had a famous one, and Cervette the younger had another. Only four double basses are known to have been made by William Forster. His commoner instruments are devoid of purfling. Ticket: "William Forster. Violin Maker in St. Martin's Lane, London."

FORSTER, WILLIAM, son of "Old" Forster. Born 1764, died 1824. He was a violin maker and repairer of some merit, but never attained the reputation of his father. He left his instruments unpurfled.

KENNEDY, ALEXANDER, came from Scotland about 1700 and established himself in London. He was a painstaking workman, and gained a good reputation. He followed the Stainer model and used a light amber varnish.

KENNEDY, JOHN, nephew and pupil of the foregoing, followed the same model, and produced some good violins and tenors.

KENNEDY, THOMAS, the best known of the family. He made a large number of violins and 'cellos.

NORMAN, BARAK (1688-1740). He was chiefly a maker of viols, but has made violas and violoncellos, and a few violins on the Stainer model; his best productions being copies of Maggini. He was probably a pupil of Urquhart, if one may judge from their respective works. As a maker of viols he was much esteemed in his day; all his instruments of this class indicate careful workmanship. As no British violoncello has been discovered anterior to those manufactured by Norman, it is thought that he may have been the first maker of that instrument in this country. They are splendid instruments and much valued. His violas also are fine specimens, and consequently highly prized by performers on that instrument. Between the years

1715 and 1720 Barak Norman entered into partnership with one Nathaniel Cross, at the sign of the
"Bass Viol," St. Paul's Churchyard. Barak resorted
to various methods in order to distinguish his instruments, sometimes his monogram is purfled in the
centre of the back, and occasionally, in the case
of violoncellos, on the top table under the wide
part of the finger-board. When he became asso-
ciated with Cross, the joint monogram was used.
The following is a copy of a printed label used by
the firm :

"Barak Norman and Nathaniel Cross, at the Bass
Viol in St. Paul's Churchyard, London, fecit 172—."

WAMSLEY, PETER, London (1727-1760).
He was at one time considered a clever maker of
violas and violoncellos, but having resorted to the
unfortunate practice of thinning the wood in his
endeavour to secure a freer tone, his instruments at
the present day lack power and sonority. They are,
however, capable of great improvement in the hands
of a skilful repairer. He adopted the Stainer model,
and at times proved himself to be a first-class workman. Most of his instruments have only ink lines

instead of purfling. Wamsley made a few double basses, but they are now very scarce. The best instruments of this maker are those covered with a dark brown varnish. For a great number of years Wamsley carried on business in Piccadilly, and used labels, copies of which are as follows :

Made by Peter Wamsley at the Harp and Hautboy in Pickadilly, 1735.

Peter Wamsley Maker at the Harp and Hautboy in Piccadilly, 17   London   51.

Made by Peter Wamſley at ÿ Golden Harp in Pickadilly London,

PART III.

ON THE DEVELOPMENT OF CLAS-
SICAL MUSIC FOR THE VIOLIN
AND OTHER STRINGED
INSTRUMENTS.

THE term "classical" as applied to music is a composition against which the destroying hand of time
has proved powerless (Riemann), in other words,
works which have been handed down to us by the
old composers, and which at the present day are
recognised as models of purity in musical art, are
now considered as classical compositions.

Coeval with that remarkable epoch when the
violin assumed its present admirable and unalter-
able form, which culminated with the closing year

of the sixteenth century, is the dawn of musical composition for the instrument, and the musicians of the
time vied with each other in producing works calculated to raise the violin from its hitherto sub-
ordinate rank as a mere accompanist to its proper
position as a solo instrument, thereby ensuring prominence and with it rapid popularity.

It is to Italy that we have to turn for any certain knowledge of the earliest classics, and the
first to claim our attention is Arcangelo Corelli
(1655-1713). He was not only the founder of
the Roman school, the earliest known, but probably the first to definitely fix the form of the
sonata. In those times two kinds of sonatas were
recognised, called respectively, *sonate da camera*,
i.e., chamber sonata, and *sonata da chiesa*, or church
sonata. The first-named consisted of a series of
dance measures (allemande, courante, saraband,
gigues, etc.), systematically arranged, whilst the
latter was a subject treated in fugal and other
learned styles, and otherwise rendered more in keeping with the dignity of the place in which such
compositions were performed. In the time of Cor-

elli, the sonata usually commenced with an *adagio*, and after two or three other movements finished with an *allegro* or *presto*.

Corelli as a composer showed a great partiality for this class of music, and his compositions rapidly spread throughout the length and breadth of Europe. Tartini caused all his pupils to study the works of Corelli. There is not, it is true, evidence of a great amount of musical erudition, but what has conferred a remarkable longevity on his works is his melodic simplicity and pure harmony. His works are forty-eight sonatas for two violins and bass (Op. 1-4), produced 1683-94; twelve sonatas for violin and bass (Op. 5), 1700; twelve "concerti-grossi," for two violins and 'cello as principal instruments, and two violins, viola and bass as accompanying instruments.

Such a gifted musician as Corelli was not likely to quit this life without leaving the impress of his artistic feelings upon those who sought his instruction, and we have ample proof of the great influence he exerted in the names of G. B. Somis (1676-1763) F. Geminiani (1680-1762), and Locatelli (1693-1764).

Somis was a close follower of his master, and it is quite easy to believe this on a comparison of their respective sonatas. Geminiani asserted more of his individuality, and this, coupled with the fact of his having received theoretical instruction from Alessandro Scarlatti, one of the most learned musicians of the day, no doubt contributed to his making a decided advance on the violin music of the time. Notwithstanding his increased knowledge as a theorist, and his greater ability as an executant, Geminiani laboured long to bring into prominence and popularity the artistic conceptions of his renowned violin master. His first effort in this direction was made in 1726 (Geminiani being then in London), when he formed Corelli's first six solos into concertos, a style of composition then recently called into existence; shortly afterwards treating another six in a similar manner. Others underwent the same process, but to these were added additional parts. Geminiani was one of the first in the field of musical expression, even sacrificing strict time to obtain it.

Locatelli furnishes us with another example, not only of the advance of technique, but of the progress

of musical culture. His works called " The Laby-
rinth," " The New Art of Modulation" and " Har-
monic Contrasts " are alone sufficient to establish him
as a great reformer in the musical world of his
time. As we have elsewhere observed, Torelli is
credited with having fixed the form of the concerto,
and a few lesser lights, such as the two Veracinis and
Alberti, live to this day by their works. The next
master whose influence marked another step in the
development of classical music for the violin was
Guiseppe Tartini (1692-1770). Here we have a
man destined for all time to stand out as one of
the most indefatigable pioneers of the violin. In
his quadruple capacity as a performer, composer,
theorist and teacher, his influence was far-reaching,
and, what is more, it has been transmitted down to
the present time. As a composer, his style of
modulation was a new thing, and his performance
came as a revelation to those who heard him for the
first time. His " Devil's Sonata " is well-known to
all violinists.

We now arrive at a name which brings us in touch
with other members of the fiddle family. Luigi

Boccherini (1740-1806), who is justly considered the father of chamber music for stringed instruments. It was he who, in 1768, gave definition to the form of the trio, the quartet and the quintet; forms which have served for the models of all subsequent composers. In the trio he was followed by Fiorillo, Cramer, Giardini, Pugnani and Viotti, and in the quartet by Mozart. His other styles were elaborated by Haydn and Beethoven. Boccherini was a prolific composer.

Three names should here be mentioned in connection with the concerto, in whose hands it underwent great improvement. They are Pugnani (1728-1798), Jarnowick (1745-1804), and Mestrino (1750-1790).

The next and last great representative of the Italian school, and one who largely influenced the French school, was Giovanni Battista Viotti (1755-1824), a pupil of Pugnani. The name of Viotti stands out with peculiar lustre, in that with him the concerto arrived at a degree of perfection hardly capable of being exceeded. The same may be said of his trios and duos, both of which should be

studied and cultivated by every young violin aspir-
ant. In Viotti the Italians have certainly produced
a fitting tailpiece to a long line of brilliant composers for the violin, a line in which no artistic hiatus
appears from the time of Corelli.

*   *   *   *   *   *

The first to establish a French school was Jean
Marie Leclair (1679-1764). Although he received
his instructions from Somis, the Italian, and became
thoroughly imbued with Italian tastes and ideas,
he laboured incessantly, on his return to France, with
the object of establishing a distinct school for his
country, and in many respects he was successful. In
1723 he published a series of solos, and soon afterwards six sonatas for two violins and bass; also
duos, trios and concertos.

The next to claim attention among the French
classical composers is Pierre Gavinies (1728-1800).
He was the first professor at the Paris Conservatoire,
then but recently formed, and the compositions he
contributed testify to considerable musical culture:
they are of great difficulty, and are, for the most
parts, sonatas and concertos.

We now introduce three names who greatly
elaborated the forms fixed by the Italians, Rode
(1774-1830), Kreutzer (1766-1831) and Baillot (1771-
1842). This almost inseparable trio are so well
known to the student, that a lengthy comment would
be superfluous. They were all in turn professors at
the Paris Conservatoire, and the joint production of
their great method for the violin, coupled with their
other educational works, place them as prominent
classical writers. Rode is known by his concertos,
caprices and airs with variations. Kreutzer's forty
studies are a household word with the earnest
student, not to mention his concertos, duets, trios
and quartets ; and the same may be said with regard
to Baillot's concertos, variations, and a host of other
pieces.

    *   *   *   *   *   *

We now pass on to consider shortly what the Ger-
mans have handed down. Like other countries, they
have been largely indebted to the Italians ; and, in
this connection, it is curious to note that with the
rise of music in Germany we find a gradual de-
cadence of the art in Italy.

In Germany we have to look to the great composers rather than the great violinists for the most important classical works for the violin.

It is unnecessary to notice anything anterior to the time of the great J. S. Bach (1685-1750); in fact, very little took place in the nature of published works.

That Bach possessed a sound perception of the capabilities and resources of the violin is amply demonstrated in all his writings for that instrument. His acquaintance with the finger-board is only excelled by his knowledge of the keyboard. Amongst the almost innumerable works of this greatest musical classic that has ever lived, I would mention his three partitas and three sonatas for violin (without accompaniment). The Chaconne in the D minor Partita is a remarkable instance of Bach's immense powers of perception.

The first real founder of a German school was Leopold Mozart (1719-1787), father of the great W. A. Mozart. He is not known by his instrumental compositions, but his claim to notice exists in the production of his "Method" for the violin, a work which not only survived several editions, but assumed the garb of several languages.

The next to call for notice is Joseph Haydn (1732-1809), a most prolific composer, especially for the string family. Attached to the service of Prince Esterhazy, a patron immensely rich and passionately fond of music, Haydn enjoyed a combination of circumstances all concurring to give opportunity for the display of his genius. It has been vouchsafed to few musicians to pursue their art under such favourable conditions as Haydn. He did not compose to please either publisher or the public. So long as his patron was satisfied with his productions, things went on merrily with him.

Let us see what Haydn did for the instrument he loved so much. Here they are—eighty-three quartets, three concertos, twenty-one trios for two violins and bass, six violin solos.

No review, however short, could lay claim to completeness without mention of the following—viz., Mozart, Weber and Beethoven. To this noble trio violinists owe much. It is, of course, quite beyond the province of this work to even enumerate the

many compositions from the pens of these immortal
musicians in which the violin took part, but I would
call attention to Beethoven's glorious Concerto in D,
Op. 61, and his two lovely Romances in G and F
respectively.

Another great German musician who exercised
considerable influence on compositions of classic
mould was Louis Spohr (1784-1859). His great
fame as a composer, combined with his reputation as
a violin virtuoso of the highest order, places him in
a conspicuous position in the history of music. The
works of Spohr are probably so well known that no
useful purpose can be served in recounting their
great merits. Suffice it to say they are of the highest
possible pitch of excellence, and require more than
ordinary technical ability to do them justice. Considered only as a composer, he has been indefatigable in the production of every style of music, and
he was especially happy in that for the strings. His
beautiful D minor Concerto is one of the finest examples of this class of music to be met with, and
its first introduction by the great master himself
made a great sensation. As one of Spohr's com-

mentators truly said, "Mozart had written solid and simple concertos, in which the performer was expected to embroider and finish the composer's sketch, and Beethoven's concertos were so written as to make the solo player merely one of the orchestra. But, as Mozart raised opera to a higher standard, so Beethoven uplifted the ideal of the orchestra, so Spohr's creative force as a violinist and writer for the violin has established the grandest school for this instrument, to which all the foremost contem·porary artists acknowledge their obligations."

Before taking leave of the German school I would mention two other names—Joseph Mayseder and Kalliwoda, both of whom contributed much that ·s good, and their works consequently attained wide popularity.

Let us now turn to our own country. We have not, it must be admitted, occupied a front rank as composers of violin music, hence the scarcity of classical works handed down to us; but let us hasten to add, we have produced the finest critics in the world, and, what is more, we are thoroughly well posted up in all the best pieces that have emanated from the thoughts of the greatest composers.

One of the earliest who wrote for the violin was one Rogers, who, in the year 1653, wrote airs in four parts for violins. He was followed by John Jenkins, who wrote twelve sonatas for two violins and a bass, printed in 1664, which were the first sonatas written by an Englishman.

James Sherard also composed several sonatas in the beginning of the last century, and they are said to bear such a resemblance to Corelli's that they might have been taken for that composer's.

The compositions of Handel materially advanced the violin in this country, and the establishment by him of Italian opera was the means of bringing us in touch with the great Italian performers and writers.

INDEX.

Addison, William, 90.
Aireton, Edmund, 91.
Albani, Matthias, 45.
———, Matthias (son), 45.
Albioni, 31.
Aldred, 11.
Amati, Andreas, 32, 46.
———, Anthony, 32, 46.
———, Hieronymus, 32, 46.
———, Nicolas, 32, 47.
Bach, 113.
Bachmann, Carl Ludwig, 72.
Baillot, 39, 112.
Baltazarini, 36, 39.
Baltzar, Tho., 23, 42.
Banks, Benjamin, 92.
———, Banjamin (son), 94.
———, James and Henry, 94.
Bannister, John, 13.
Barrett, John, 95.
Beethoven, 110, 115.
Benda, Francis, 43.
Bente, 32, 72.
Bergonzi, Carlo, 48.
———, Michael Angelo, 49.
Betts, John, 95.
Boccherini, Luigi, 109.
Bolles, 11.
Boquay, Jacques, 83.
Buchstetter, Gabriel David, 72.
———, Josephus, 73.
Buddiani, 32.
Cappa, Giofredo, 49.
Cervette, 100.
Chanot, François, 87.
Chaucer, 15.
Choron, 37.
Cole, Thomas, 90.
Corelli, A., 28, 31, 106.
Corette, Michael, 37.

Cramer, William, 43, 110.
Cross, Nathaniel, 101.
Crossdill, 100.
De Beriot, 39.
Dodd, Thomas, 97.
Dubourg, 42.
Duke, Richard, 97.
Eberle, Ulric, 73.
Feltham, Owen, 16.
Fendt, Bernhard, 97.
Fétis, 2.
Forster, William, 97.
———, William (son), 100.
Gagliano, Allessandro, 50.
———, Antonio, 51.
———, Ferdinando, 51.
———, Genaro, 50.
———, Giovanni, 51.
———, Guiseppe, 51.
———, Nicolas, 51.
———, Raffael, 51.
Gavinies, Pierre, 39, 111.
Geminiani, F., 28, 34, 107-8.
Giardini, 35, 110.
Grancino, Giovanni Battista, 52.
———, Paolo, 52.
Guadagnini, Giovanni Battista, 53.
———, Guiseppe, 53.
———, Lorenzo, 52.
Guarnerius, Andreas, 54.
———, Guiseppe, 53.
———, Joseph, 32, 55.
———, Pietro, 58.
Guhr, 43.
Habeneck, 39.
Handel, 117.
Haydn, 110, 114.

Helmer, Charles, 73.
Hoffmann, Martin, 73.
Jarnowick, 34, 110.
Jauch (Jaug), 74.
Jay, 10.
Jenkins, John, 117.
Kennedy, Alexander, 100.
———, John, 100.
———, Thomas, 101.
Kiesewetter, 43.
Klotz, Egidius, 74.
——— family, 44, 74.
———, Mathias, 75.
———, Sebastian, 75.
Kreutzer, 39, 112.
Lafont, 39.
Lahousaye, 39.
Landolphus, Carlo, 59.
Leclair, Jean Marie, 39, 111.
Lindley, Robert, 100.
Locatelli, 107-8.
Lott, John Frederick, 97.
Lully, J. B., 36.
Lupot, François, 87.
———, Nicholas, 40, 85.
Mace, Thomas, 10.
Maggini, Giovanni Paolo, 32, 59.
———, Pietro Sancto, 32.
Marietto, 31.
Mariani, 32.
Mayseder, 43.
Mell, Davis, 25.
Mestrino, 34, 110.
Molique, 43.
Montagnani, Dominic, 61.
Mozart, Leopold, 43.
———, W. A., 110.
Norman, Barak, 101.
Otto, 80.
Paganini, 58.
Pamphilon, Edward, 90
Peacham, 17.
Pemberton, 90.
Pepys, 26.

Playford, John, 7.
Pugnani, 35, 110.
Rauch, Thomas, 76.
Rayman, Jacob, 91.
Reade, Charles, 33.
Rode, 39, 112.
Rogers, 117.
Ross, 11.
Rugeri, Francesco, 62.
———, Giambatista, 62.
Ruppert, 76.
Salo, Gasparo da, 13, 32, 63.
Scheinlein, Matthias Frederick, 77.
Seraphin, Sanctus, 64.
Sherard, James, 31.
Smith, 11.
Solomon, J., 43.
Somis, G. B., 107.
Spohr, Louis, 43, 115.
Stainer, Jacobus, 43, 77.
Stamitz, John, 43.
Storioni, Lorenzo, 65.
Stradivarius, Antonius, 28, 32, 65.
———, Francesco, 69.
———, Omobono, 69.
Strutt, 14.
Tartini, Guiseppe, 31, 34, 109.
Techler, David, 70.
Testore, Carlo Antonio, 71.
———, Carlo Guiseppe, 71.
———, Paolo Antonio, 71.
Torelli, 31.
Tywersus, 40.
Urquhart, 90.
Valentini, 31.
Veracini, 28.
Viotti, 34, 110.
Vuillaume, John Baptiste, 40, 87.
Wamsley, Peter, 102.
Weber, 115.
Wise, Christopher, 90.
Wood, Anthony, 18.